WEST SULLIVAN DAYS

Recollections of Growing Up
in a Tiny Maine Village

by
Jack Havey

Printed at Versa Press, East Peoria, IL

2   4   6   8   7   5   3   1

ISBN 0-89272-509-5

Library of Congress Control Number: 2001090322

DOWN EAST BOOKS
Camden, Maine
www.downeastbooks.com
Book Orders: (800) 685-7962

❧ CONTENTS ☙

❧ CONTENTS ❧

(continued)

∾ PREFACE ঙ৹

Many characteristics contribute to making "down east" Maine the very special place that it is. To the lasting annoyance of the folks who live there, one of those is that most people don't know where the region actually is.

And that's important only as it relates to where it isn't.

For example, a Bostonian headed for Ogunquit Beach (in southernmost Maine) speaks of going "down east" for the weekend—enough to give a true down-easter a straight-out rash.

For the geographically curious, down east is neither Kennebunkport, nor Portland, nor Cape Elizabeth, Scarborough, Yarmouth, Falmouth, nor all of the above combined. Fortunately, if you're driving east of, say, Belfast along the Maine coast, there are ways to find out whether you're down east or not. One reliable test is the so-called "small-store check." Begin stopping at little grocery stores and asking for "strip fish." If the clerk gives you a blank stare—one that suggests that you just stepped off the banana boat—well, you're not even close to where you want to be.

On the other hand, if you get a smile and a bundle of dried, salted fish strips wrapped in waxed white butcher paper, then you're in the ballpark.

But for sure, when you do get there, there won't be a painted line on the road or a big sign that announces you have arrived down east. You'll just have to sense the difference, beginning with villages that sound, smell, and look well beaten upon. You'll find houses that have been handed down again and again over the years within a single family. You'll witness raw, scenic beauty that's deeper and richer in its colors than what you've seen along the shore in the southern and mid-coast regions of Maine. You'll enter small towns that are obviously populated by hard-driven, independent families who have fished the local waters, worked the woods, and raked the blueberry fields and clam flats for generations.

If you like what you find, and if you decide to become part of one of this region's communities, it may take the passing of several springs before those people will spare the time to judge how you pull—or fail to pull—your own weight.

Fencing-in this spectacular part of the world are its islands. There are hundreds and hundreds of sparkling outcroppings hereabouts, ranging from stony ledge tops that disappear with the rising tide, to more magnificent land masses that house entire year-round communities. Some of these islands have descriptive names like Egg Rock, Great Duck, and Double Shot, while others lean to the historic—Petit Manan, Bois Bubert, and Isle au Haut. Each has its own special texture of rock and vegetation, nurtured by the penetration and endurance of a fog that rarely sleeps.

For excitement, most every town has its general store, well stocked with anything you'd ever need or want, including some of the best storytellers east of Ellsworth Falls. Without their brand of humor, without the caring and special bonding among all who live there, down east Maine would be a lonely stretch of land and sea.

West Sullivan Days is my own remembrance of growing up down east. Writing it was a mental exercise filled with excitement. Imagine: You're seventy-plus years old and you surer-than-hell have passed the clubhouse turn, but you challenge your mind to reach back decades, for names and details that have been asleep under dust for years. For one who can't remember where in the supermarket parking lot he left his car, that challenge was truly a stimulating and rewarding adventure.

If one of the stories within takes you back to an experience you had when you were younger, I hope it was a good one.

Jack Havey
Winthrop, Maine

❧ 1 ❧

Chickens, Cigars, and Ragtime Music

The only thing that stood between our family home in West Sullivan and the town baseball field was Route 1. You knew it was Route 1 because right at the end of our graveled driveway was one of those official-looking, black-and-white signs with the numeral one painted on it. We weren't impressed and just called it "the main road."

There were times when things could get very, very exciting—like the day the chicken truck from Calais tipped over right in front of our place. Thousands and thousands of white chickens got loose from their cages and were running all over the ballfield, pecking on our lawn, and walking right up and down the middle of the road. Everybody in town was there.

Well, Wayne Mills was there, but he wasn't. He was drunk and asleep in the back of Eddy Crosby's Ford. Eddy and Junior Bunker caught nine of those chickens, put them in the back seat, and drove off. The next day at the post office they reported that Wayne slept with those chickens all night long.

The Havey family home was a hundred-year-old farmhouse with a rambling, screened-in porch that looked out across the ballfield to the Taunton, a tidal river that changed directions every six hours and emptied (or filled, depending on the tide) just below the falls at Frenchman Bay. The main house connected to a long, low shed that connected to the barn that connected to dozens of swallow nests whose occupants zoomed in and out through the barn doors from the beginning to the end of summer. The house sat on thirty acres of field and woodland, and it stayed in the family until my father sold it for back taxes in the early forties. The amount was about thirty-five hundred dollars.

My great grandparents had lived there, raising five sons, any one of whom my great grandmother always said she would rather see, "coming up the driveway in a casket before seeing him walk up the drive smoking a cigar." Which pretty much identified her as being a hundred years or so ahead of her time.

But after she passed away, one of her sons, Harvard Hannah Havey, my grandfather, was the next generation to live there, and he was a cigar smoker of considerable renown. His habit didn't bother his wife, as long as he refrained from "bringing the filthy things in the house." He obliged.

That may have been the harshest dictum that Martha Moore Havey ever issued to Harvard or anyone else. A beautiful lady just under six feet tall, she stood straight as

Wayne slept with those chickens all night long.

a ramrod. She and Gramp raised two sons of their own—as different as two brothers could be. But couldn't those boys play piano! Neither Barney Morton Havey nor his younger brother, Dwight, ever had a lesson at the keyboard. But jazz, ragtime—you name it—they could handle any request at the drop of the hat.

In the mid-twenties, Barney Morton requested the hand of Marjorie Malkson, a young sweetheart from down in Washington County, and they brought me into the act a few years later. My brother, Bill, joined us five years after that, and we became the last bunch of Haveys to occupy the old family home.

As a fella said, " It warn't always easy, but it was better than fallin' on a sharp rock."

2

Buicks and Bikes

The big green house over to the left of our place had a front porch so high that you could jump off it and break your ankle—in addition to getting all scratched up in the rambling rose bush. Uncle Dwight, Aunt Zelda, and my cousins, Keith and Jody, lived there, and every one of them could play piano and guitar. They could sing, too, and would harmonize sweetly when they did "Red River Valley." I'd join along.

Stored up on blocks in an old garage out behind their barn was a 1925 Buick that people claimed would never ever run again because, "They don't make belts for 'em no more." But on any rainy day, I could get her up to forty-eight miles per hour, and Keith, who was two years older, could get her up to fifty. Jody never drove because she was scared the car would start.

In back of the garage Uncle Dwight raised a hog every year, and did that animal ever stink!

Connecting the two houses—theirs and ours—was a well-beaten path. Six hundred and thirty-seven steps long from either direction, it went straight through the field.

You could bike it real fast, and generally the first one on the path won. Even Keith couldn't get his bike by you in that high grass. Now, a footrace was something else, because Jody could leg it through the stuff like it was nothing.

If a bike ever needed air in its tires, Bobby Black's Garage was only a ways down from Dwight's, but my mother never let me go there. "Those boys just don't look clean, and they swear a lot. Plus, your father doesn't want you riding that thing on the main road." (Yeah, Ma, and you left out the part about the Mack truck calendar in Bobby's office.)

Bobby could drive a vehicle faster than everybody else in town. And after he'd do a brake job, he'd test the car by driving it up the main road wide-open and slamming the brakes right to the floorboard. There'd be a long screeching sound, along with the smell of burning rubber. And people—especially my mother—would take notice, as in, "What's he trying to do out there now, kill everybody?!?" Right, Ma.

Nope, if I needed air in my bike tires I had to take it over to Jimmy, "who speaks well of everyone," at Dickens's Garage. It was twice as far and twice as hard to get to. But my protests—"Honest, Ma, the guys over there swear twice as much"—fell on deaf ears.

✌ 3 ✌

Hayin' with Harnden and the Hannahs

Point-of-fact, exercise was never hard to come by in West Sullivan—or, I'm sure, anyplace in Maine during the years when I was growing up. I worked in the fields as a gofer for Mrs. Hannah's three "boys," Alden, Moon, and Harnden. Harnden Hannah was in his forties, and his brothers weren't that far behind.

Neither Alden nor Harnden ever spoke much, even to one another, but Moon always got me laughing. I was never quite sure whether he was trying to or not. The work was hard but had its rewards. If you've never been hayin' on a boiling hot summer's day, and if you've never tasted ice-cold weak tea with a lot of sugar, straight out of a tin bucket, letting it run out of the sides of your mouth and down your face, well then you've never tasted.

Mrs. Hannah, bless her heart, deducted the first Social Security payment of my life from my earnings. I was eight years old, and she said she was sorry to have to do it. My old man snorted, "Just what I told you, that's what the hell FDR's all about." But at pay time, on Saturday, Mrs.

Hannah would give us a plate of the hottest, best biscuits in the world to share, and I always wished I could stay around and have dinner with the "boys." Her kitchen was always pleasant. There was a big, round table with a red-and-white oilcloth table cover, straight out of J. J. Newberry's five-and-dime. And the memorable smell of baked beans and bread in the oven blended with the aroma of fresh milk and cows out in the barn.

All too soon the horn on my mother's '35 Chevy coupe would beep outside, and I would remember that riding home in the rumble seat, with that nice breeze coming cool off the river, was pretty fine, too.

Trouble was, when we got home I had to turn over my pay to my mother. Don't get me wrong. She was the nicest, most beautiful mother a kid could have. She loved me, my brother, and my father dearly. But she was a tightwad. I mean, since FDR took part of my paycheck, did the rest really have to go for school clothes? Every Saturday she'd say, "We'll just put part of this away, and come fall you can pick out whatever you want." Yeah, like corduroy knickers and a sweater!

But if my mother played her nickels and dimes close to the vest, she certainly let loose when it came to passing out encouragement to anyone in need of it. She was a God-loving person who never preached but led by example. Not uncommonly, I would wake up at sunrise, go to the kitchen table, and draw pictures on any piece of paper available. She'd come down maybe an hour later, look at my hen scratches, pick out one, and say, "This is beautiful. May I have it?" I'd sign it for her, and years later I found many, many of my early "pieces of art" in a box she had tucked away.

❧ 4 ❧

The Tastes
(and Smells) of Summer

It was a muggy July morning, and Shirley Clemmons was sitting on the post-office steps with his Lab, Georgia, waiting for the mail truck to arrive from Ellsworth.

Jimmy Dickens had just opened up his garage and was behind his wooden desk, trying to figure out the receipts made out by Wayne "Ding" Mills. Ding had covered for him the day before while Jimmy took his wife, Florence, shopping in Bangor. Ding was in the toilet. He had slept there all night after killing a pint of Southern Comfort at the East Sullivan Grange Hall dance. In a little while, as usual, he'd come out, slop cold water on his stubbled face, and step over to the soda cooler to "put out the fire." Then, he'd commence to down one bottle of pop right after another. Ding never swallowed when he drank. He'd just tilt the bottle back and let the contents drain straight down his throat.

The thing I always wondered about, though, was whether his pants were going to stay on or drop off. They were always black and oily, and just about the time you thought for sure they were going south, he'd give 'em a hoist.

The fish market was across the main road from Jimmy's Garage, smack dab on the right as you came off the Hancock/Sullivan bridge. Oscar "Oc" Gordon owned it, operated it, and was the sole catcher of all the fish, clams, and lobsters sold there. It was a one-room place about ten feet square, with a cement floor that you could hose down easily. There was a small counter but no cash register; the money always stayed in a snap-pouch, tucked in Oc's pocket.

That morning, I pulled up in front of the market and got off my bike promptly at seven o'clock. Right away I could smell the strong odor of dead herring that we would use for bait in the lobster traps. Oc grabbed up the bait bucket, and we went down the really steep embankment to the pound, where the boat was tied along the riverbank. He walked with great, long strides; I ran alongside trying to keep up.

Oc was a tall, rangy man with tremendous hands. When he took off his ball cap, his head showed two halves: a brown, sun-worn face and a white-as-a-baby's-butt, balding skull. He always had a chew of Red Man, even while sucking his pipe. And he always wore hip boots, rolled down below the knee. Oc was one of my first heroes and, in retrospect, I sure would love to have been able to paint strong portraits back then. This was a very strong man.

*Oc grabbed up the bait bucket and walked with great,
long strides; I ran alongside trying to keep up.*

His round-bottomed, wooden boat was always in need of a fresh coat of green paint. It was rigged with a very small gasoline motor, but that morning Oc shoved off and moved out into the river's tide using just the oars. I guarded the bait bucket full of dead herring.

Around nine o'clock it started to get wicked hot on the river. Oc reached under his seat and slid out a beat-up cardboard box with "Morton's Salt" and the slogan, "when it rains, it pours" printed on the sides. Inside the box were a few empty bottles and one reasonably cool-looking stubby of Genesee Ale. Oc held it in one hand and removed the top with the other. It was not a twist-off.

"Bring anything to drink, Jackie?" he asked. I told him I hadn't but said that I'd had home brew before, stuff my father made in the bathtub. He took a slash of the ale and passed me the bottle. "Wet your whistle," he said, "but better you don't tell Marjie [my mother], or this could be our last run at it."

There's a special excitement about lobstering. Every haul is like Christmas morning 'cause you never know what's waiting in that trap below until you just about have it pulled onto the boat. Could it be a forty-eight pounder like the one Duke Tracey pulled out of Frenchman Bay? Or just a few starfish, with a bunch of snails hanging on for the ride? That's the thing: you just never know.

That particular morning, Oc pulled the traps by hand with me helping by rebaiting each one with that stinking dead herring. In all, we brought back ten, pound to pound-

and-a-half lobsters from a total of seventy-five traps, which isn't a lot of gear by today's standards. As I learned on my first time out, even on a calm, beautiful July day it takes a lot of guts to be a lobsterman. Dead herring guts.

Oscar would sell our catch in the market for twenty-five cents each—maybe "five for a dollar" if he'd had a snort or two. Course, the price was always higher for the Summer People. It was a hoot to watch them come into the place. The fish market was always open all day long, and Oc might be there or he might not. He could be at the post office just jawing it up. Anyone in town knew that if his Dodge pickup wasn't around, he wasn't either.

But the Summer People never figured that out, and they talked so much and so fast, they could be in the market for twenty minutes before realizing they weren't being waited on. With a little luck, Ding or someone over at the garage might yell out, "He's gone to a funeral." The Summer People'd walk away muttering, "Don't people here in Maine know enough to lock their doors?"

Why? Did we need to?

❧ 5 ☙

The World's Strongest Man

Duke Tracey's house sat on the corner of the mile-long Track Road, which was all sand, ruts, and gravel, and the road to North Sullivan, which was tarred and ran all the way up to Franklin. It was a tiny little place—three, maybe four rooms—with an exterior of weathered shingles that had endured more than their share of down-east winters. It sat on granite slabs from the quarry up in North Sullivan.

Being the man-of-the-world that he was, Duke traveled around the whole state of Maine—mostly with carnivals—selling tickets, running wheel games, and, in general, just doing his own thing. So his mother lived in the West Sullivan house alone, except for those times when Duke would come back to visit. Mrs. Tracey was normally at home, but it was hard to tell because the front door, which had no screen, was always shut, and the green shades in the windows were pretty much pulled down all the time.

For all these reasons, the most exciting man in the

town of West Sullivan—and maybe in the whole state of Maine—was rarely seen. But the house became something of a landmark just the same.

If an out-of-towner was seeking directions to the Tracey home, an event that would have been rare indeed, he'd probably end up at the West Sullivan post office, located diagonally across the road. And there, Postmaster Shirley Clemmons and his wife, Audry, held court twice a day (except Sundays) before a wide range of liars and self-made comedians who were ostensibly there to get their mail.

Except for the *Ellsworth American,* which came in on Fridays, our own mail normally consisted of bills addressed to my grandfather's granite business: Crabtree & Havey Company; H. H. Havey, Treasurer; North Sullivan; Maine. Since Gramps had been dead for years, and Crabtree & Havey had gone into bankruptcy years before that, getting these past-due invoices annoyed the hell out of my mother.

Her instructions to the messenger (me) stayed pretty consistent over the years, "Tell that Shirley Clemmons to put this Crabtree & Havey stuff in Dwight's box. What am I supposed to do with it?!" And once in a while, if I was mad at my mother, I'd say, "It wasn't Shirley. It was Audry," and then she'd really be ticked off.

The post office was filled with a dozen or so smoothly worn wooden chairs, and Shirley always filled the one by the stove—nicely filled, you might say. In addition to sorting the mail into little combination-lock boxes, the Clemmonses sold bread and milk and penny candy— providing Audry hadn't eaten it all, particularly the licorice. "She does have a sweet tooth," my mother would say. Which was a lot nicer than what Audry said when my mother sent me back to the post office with a loaf of bread that she didn't feel, was "all that fresh."

But it was more than just close proximity that connected the Tracey home and the West Sullivan post office. There was the legend himself.

Since Duke Tracey and Shirley Clemmons had grown up together, Duke would always drop the postmaster a card to let him know when he was coming home. And that, of course, was like telling everybody in town— including Mrs. Tracey, who didn't read all that much. "Duke'll be home on Monday," Shirley'd say, and you could feel the excitement.

Everybody'd be sitting there listening to Oc Gordon telling about "the biggest jesusly buck I ever seen. I ain't saying where I saw it but . . ." and in would walk Duke. Now, he was no John Wayne kind of Duke, and the room wouldn't go silent. Someone might say, "Hey, Duke, how they hangin'?" but Oc would finish lying about the "biggest jesusly buck." There'd be a few handshakes, and the next thing you knew Duke would be sitting there laughing it up and in general acting as if he was no different from any of them. But he was. Even my Uncle Dwight, who rarely dropped by the post office, would make the trip just to see the man he had named his favorite hunting dog after.

You see, Duke Tracey was the strongest man in the world.

Don't believe it? Then just you ask anyone in town, mister man!

Don't believe it? Just compare Duke with Charles Atlas, the guy in those magazine ads where he claimed he used to be a ninety-eight-pound weakling.

Don't believe it? Then just you waltz yourself up to the post office while Duke's home and watch him bend a one-inch-thick, ten-inch-long steel railroad spike right in two—and tear the thickest phone book straight through the middle.

Then, knock on the door over at Duke's house, and ask his mother if you can go into the kitchen and see the forty-eight-pound lobster mounted on the wall, the one Duke caught in Frenchman Bay with his bare hands!

The only thing that wasn't strong about him was his eyes. He always wore "coke bottle" glasses (my father claimed Duke had syphilis from running around with "all those carnival tramps" when he was a kid). In fact, the night Dwight took all of us over to Hancock Point to see Duke wrestle Man Mountain Green, I hardly recognized him without the spectacles.

But he didn't have any problem at all finding Man Mountain. Duke caught him by his shorts and threw him out of the ring after Man Mountain tried a choke hold.

Duke Tracy was the strongest man in the world.

Duke always called me, "Jackie dear," which is a term of fondness even among the men down east. When I was nine years old, I painted a portrait of him from memory. And I'm sure what the painting lacked in talent it made up for in muscles. I made them huge. During the next six or seven years I would see Duke off and on until I joined the marines. After that, I didn't see him again until the early '60s. Then, while walking my daughters around the Winthrop Beach fairgrounds, I heard, "Jackie dear, who you got there?"

It was the legend himself. Duke came out from behind his gaming booth, picked up the girls as if they were feathers, and gave them both big hugs.

Yessir, he was the strongest man in the world. And one of the nicest.

❧ 6 ❧

School Days

The Lindseys and the Jewetts, who had twenty-one and fourteen kids, respectively, lived right next to the town ballpark, directly across the main road from Dwight's house and slightly downwind from us. Poor as church mice, they made their living at logging. They'd cut and saw up cordwood for people who had timber in exchange for a small share for themselves. They would sell off some of this wood and stack the rest of it outside their kitchens for winter fuel.

Buddy Jewett was one of my best friends. At nine years old, although he was shorter than me, Buddy was nothing but a ripple of muscles, one on top of the other. He was the youngest in the family; the closest to him was his brother Guy, who was nineteen. Mr. Jewett looked old enough to be my grandfather. Sort of a spread-out group of minifamilies, you might say, all living in the same ramshackle house.

Their kitchen had a few cupboards, a woodstove, and a dirt floor. If you sat in there too long, your eyes would water and really burn—and you'd always come out smelling like smoke.

My mother loved Guy. Actually, she loved the whole family, because they were "honest and always reliable." She would declare, "All the Jewetts have beautiful teeth, and they just use salt and soda!"

For twenty-five cents an hour, Guy would do chores that my father had left for my mother during the week— like unplugging the septic pipe, a job that she wasn't too hot about doing. On those days, Guy would come in for his noon break, and my mother would serve him a cold glass of grape Kool-Aid, a tunafish sandwich, and (if there were any left) a Fig Newton cookie. After he left, the kitchen would smell like woodsmoke for a day or so. But who cared? Guy didn't drink, didn't smoke, didn't curse, and never bragged. He was just one nice guy!

Buddy and I sat next to each other in school, and every year at lice time he'd have his head shaved clean, as would the rest of the Jewetts and all the Lindseys. It would strike me, particularly with the Lindseys, that they all looked alike. In fact, even when their hair grew back, they still all looked alike, the girls and the boys.

Buddy would sit there and scratch, and then I'd start scratching—"sympathy itching," my mother called it. But "just in case," I'd get a tar-soap shampoo every night, right there in the kitchen, in the set tubs where she did the laundry.

Our grammar school was a large, old, two-room schoolhouse. It had a big, dusty playground with a swing, a furnace that smoked, and no running water. As in, no flush toilets. Miss Bradford, who was the first raving beauty of a woman I had ever known, taught the first, second, third, fourth, and fifth grades in one room. Fresh out of Farmington State Normal School, she was slim with long legs, dark hair, and dark eyes. She reminded me of Lil' Abner's girlfriend, Abbey, in Al Capp's comic strip. She boarded at Mrs. Gerrish's house, right across the road from the school.

Mr. Hinckley, who thought he looked like Boston Blackie, the radio private eye, taught the sixth and seventh grades in the other room.

Being in the third grade, Buddy and I sat up front, in row three. Miss Bradford would teach one grade, give them some "homework," and move along the rows of desks to the next grade. Obviously, we were free to listen to the teaching going on in the other grades, and I liked to brag that I could already do fifth-grade math. And I could. Which may have been the high point of my formal education.

The low point was what I remember as "the day of embarrassment." Keep in mind that one of my great pleasures was to see how fast I could do my homework. When I finished, I would raise my hand 'til I got Miss Bradford's attention, then ask that I be able to go to the closet for a piece of construction paper. With my request granted, I would get one, then return to my desk and draw essentially the same landscape I had done the day before—and the day before that: There was a big cliff on one side of the sheet, a big cliff on the other side, and water in between.

But on this particular day, I got a little carried away with my drawing. The first plane appeared in the sky with machine guns blazing, *brrrrrrr, brrrrrrr.* Suddenly, a submarine showed up in the water. Bomb it! *Wheeeeeee . . . kaboom!* Missed. Drop another one! *Wheeeeeee . . . kaboom!* Bring out the U.S. Army on one cliff and the Germans on the other side. Fire the artillery! *Berrrroom! Berrrroom!* Okay, cease fire, men.

I was unaware what was going on behind me until I sensed Miss Bradford standing there. The room had become dead quiet. "What ever are you doing, Jack?" she asked.

"I'm drawing, ma'am," I replied. "You gave me permission, remember?"

"Okay," she said, patting my head, "But can we keep the cannon fire down to a dull roar, please?" The whole room shook with whooping laughter. I've never forgotten it or lived it down.

But that wasn't the end of what turned out to be a very memorable day.

Since our house was over a mile from the school, the school bus always stopped at the end of the driveway. In the morning we'd ride, but we generally hiked home in the afternoon. That way, among other things, we could stop by the Alhambra theater and see if there were any new movie posters up—Victor McLaughlin in *The Last*

Legionnaire, Tom Mix, Gene Autry, or maybe Hopalong Cassidy. Anybody but the dreaded Nelson Eddy and Jeanette MacDonald. She singing up a storm, he on the other side of the woods in his Canadian Mountie uniform, singing back. It was enough to make a third-grader vomit.

The Bukers lived just a few houses down from the Alhambra, and on this particular day Buddy Jewett had stopped by to spend some time with Earlon Buker, who was in the next grade up from us. Mrs. Buker was generally "away sick," and Earlon spent a lot of time at home alone. Mr. Buker kept a wide range of guns in the house, and Buddy and Earlon took great interest in a pistol, which they used to play out a robbery scene. When Earlon pointed the piece at Buddy and pulled the trigger, they both thought the gun was empty. It wasn't.

Mrs. Gerrish, who luckily was driving somewhere, found Buddy lying by the road in a pool of his own blood, not too far from the Buker house, with a gaping gunshot wound in his chest. Dr. Black (no relation to Bobby Black) later said that the bullet, which had come out the other side, had just missed Buddy's left lung. The doctor declared, "He's goddam lucky!"

We all were, because although Buddy was a Jewett, he was also a jewel.

7

Gawd, I Wish I'd Had a Camera

If Eastport, Maine, is the first town in the United States to catch the sun every morning, my bedroom in West Sullivan, about eighty miles to the southwest as the crow flies, must have come in a close second. And with the first sliver of light that passed through the window, I'd be up on my elbow checking out the river, which would be cloudy and rough on one kind of day, and sunny and flat on my kind of day. This one just happened to be my kind of day—bright and calm with just a nip of early November in the air.

On the other hand, things weren't about to go all that sunny and rosy-bright up at Arthur Bunker's slaughter-house, where my Cousin Keith was starting his first day on the job. Keith was ten. Arthur Bunker was his grandfather, on Zelda's side of the family.

Ever since he'd been a tiny kid, Keith had always watched Dwight dress deer and other wildlife, so all the blood and guts stuff wasn't about to faze him. Nor did he have any problem helping Mr. Bunker pull that live, golden brown calf out of the old closed-in truck and drag it down the rickety wooden ramp to be butchered. (Whenever we'd see that same truck going down the road, we'd yell out, "Dead cow. Dead pig. Arthur Bunker does the jig." I mean, he wasn't *my* grandfather.)

The trouble developed when Keith went to help push the ramp back onto the truck. He let go of the rope attached to the calf's halter.

Now, the slaughterhouse was on the ground floor of a humongous three-story barn, framed with great beams that were held in place with rugged wooden pegs. It sat on top of a twenty-foot embankment, looking directly down onto the river. The main house was higher up on the hillside, and on this day—as always—Mable Bunker, Arthur's wife, had been up cooking and baking since three in the morning. Later, these baked goods would go into Arthur's other meat truck, a small Dodge, and he would peddle them door-to-door.

It was now seven o'clock, and Mable was taking her first real break of the day. Sitting in that huge kitchen, her pans covering the woodstove and the smell of fresh pies and baked bread surrounding her, she stared out the window and sipped a cup of hot coffee with four sugars. Just as she was starting to relax, that calf went scooting by her window like a shot-outta-hell. Non too nimble, Mable did manage to get to the back door just as Keith and his grandfather came running and puffing up the steep road from the slaughterhouse.

"Arthur," she yelled, "is that calf loose?" It was, of course, and what happened next would later bring tears to the eyes of all the ol' boys at the post office.

Across the way, Dottie Grindall was out on her front lawn beating the sand and dust out of her kitchen carpet. She took in the whole fracas and would later say, "Gawd, I wish I'd had a camera." Of course, Dottie normally said, "Gawd, I wish I'd had a camera," about nine times a day, whether the event was something worthy of a picture or not. Take the time her sister got locked out of the car while she was over in Ellsworth shopping. Okay, maybe that was worth a, "Gawd, I wish I'd had a camera." But Mabel's seeing Ding Mills having a hard time opening a bottle of soda pop? No. Hardly a photo-op, even for Dottie.

In any event, not far away, Leslie Goodwin stepped out of the woods and into the field right where he had left his pickup earlier that morning, at the upper end of the Track Road. He sat on the running board, rolled a little Edgeworth into a cigarette paper, licked the length of the paper, stuck it together, and lit up. Since daybreak, Leslie had made a circle of about ten miles—up toward North Sullivan, close to Franklin, and back. It was a nice, calm morning with that special smell of fall in the woods, but there had been no deer in sight. He had flushed a few partridge, seen a young fox, and kicked out two rabbits. But no deer. Now, as he sat there on his pickup, snot dripping off the end of his nose and the sun hitting him warm in the face, Leslie wondered whether he should make one more circle or pack it in 'til late afternoon.

That's when he heard the crunching of dried twigs and leaves about seventy yards away, right near an old crabapple tree. He rose quietly to a standing position, and that's when he first saw the doe's head.

He thought, "Do I really want to squander my deer tag away on a doe?" All summer long Leslie had harbored visions of something like a ten-point, 240-pound buck. On the other hand, if he could nail this doe, cover it up in the back of the truck, and get it home without running into anyone, particularly Warden Barrett . . . What the hell, he'd give it a go. The doe hadn't moved, Leslie raised his .300 Savage and pow! dropped it with one clean shot through the neck.

The crack of the rifle was in almost perfect sync with the sound of Arthur Bunker's old, green truck grinding it up the Track Road.

"You be deer hunting?" Arthur asked, as he stepped down.

Leslie was pissed. "I be shooting a doe," he replied sarcastically and gestured over toward the crabapple tree. When Arthur said that he and Keith would give Leslie a hand pulling the deer through the field to the pickup, they all walked over to the tree.

It's never a happy moment when what you thought you were shooting turns out to be something else entirely— especially when it's a dead calf with a rope around its neck. But Arthur Bunker was good. He commiserated with

Leslie, saying, "Well, somebody had to do it."

It was eight, maybe ten days before Leslie Goodwin ventured into the post office. The afternoon chatter was heavy, and it was about five minutes before Eddy Crosby yelled across the room to Junior Bunker. "Hey Jun," he asked, "D'ya hear about the ol' boy down in Gouldsboro that goes in the woods, ropes his deer, then walks it out to his truck before he shoots it?"

As Dottie Grindall would say, "Gawd, I wish I'd had a camera."

❧ 8 ❧

Tunk Lake

"On a clear day," Maynard Young was saying, "you can read the front page of the *Bangor Daily,* straight down through ten feet of water."

He was exaggerating only slightly about Tunk Lake, which is really a lake and a pond—Big Tunk and Little Tunk. Lying at the base of Caribou Mountain, Big Tunk's clear, pristine waters run nearly three hundred feet deep and have long been home to some of Maine's finest landlocked salmon. Separated from its more imposing sibling by a few acres of timberland, Little Tunk is very shallow. Here, you can "fly-fish only" for brookies (Eastern brook trout). Neither body of water is very accessible, and I'm not saying how you get in there.

My dad knew how, but that was about the limit of his "outdoorsmanship." Barney Morton, "Mort," Havey was the editor of an evening newspaper in Bangor and an excellent writer. He was not a fisherman. But on this particular winter weekend, Mort decided he'd go ice fishing. And he'd take me. And my Uncle Wally. And my Cousin Bob. Uncle Wally, it was well known, didn't know diddly about fishing, either. He was a band leader at night, normally slept all day, and rarely even saw the out-of-doors.

We loaded up the Ford, pulled out of the yard in West Sullivan, and headed for Tunk. Lucky for us, there was no snow, and the ground was frozen. So we managed the back roads all the way into Sue and Chief Stanwoods' camps without getting stuck. In those days, save for the Stanwoods' own dwellings and the three rickety cabins that they rented out, there was only one other place on either lake. A huge log home about halfway up Big Tunk, it was owned and occupied (summers only) by Admiral Richard Byrd, American naval officer and polar explorer.

After unloading a knapsack and several cardboard boxes of food from the Ford and carrying them into our designated cabin, Wally appointed himself to make "one beauty of a fire" in the small fireplace. It was zero weather outside, but the camp had been warmed by the woodstove that Sue had going for us. Still, a fire in the fireplace seemed like an all right idea. The only thing all wrong was letting Wally build it. Quicker than you could say "by the old Lord Harry," the place was alive with thick smoke.

We opened the door. Closed the door. Let the smoke out. Let the cold air in. By the time Chief Stanwood arrived (note that he was not a fire chief but an Indian chief) and managed to reach into the fireplace and open up the flue, we had frozen our collective asses off. "Oh, so that's the trick," Wally observed.

Once our eyes stopped burning and the place started to

warm up a tad, Wally announced, "Dinner's coming right up," and he broke out the bacon and eggs. He and my dad also broke out a half-gallon of wine, plus some hard stuff Wally had brought along in a silver flask. We all turned in after supper, and not long after that, the fires were dead out. So again, even in our long underwear, we froze our collective asses off.

Wally was not eager to brave the outdoors, but he did. He got up in the middle of the night, pulled on his boots, and went out to relieve himself. Whereupon he managed to pee all over his long johns, which, in turn, froze up tighter than a woodpecker's beak. This was not going to be one trip Wally would write home about.

But for me, at only eight, the next day out on Big Tunk was gonna be a big one. I was going to learn how to drive the car. Let Wally teach his kid how to fish—my dad was gonna teach me how to drive, by Jeezus!

We woke up to find the morning sunny but still wicked cold. We all jumped in the Ford and rode across the ice about halfway up Big Tunk—carrying provisions, kindling for the outdoor "campfire," and ice-fishing gear.

On the day we left West Sullivan, Mort and Wally had been given an ice-fishing lesson by Rodney Ash, who ran the bait shop where we stopped and bought live smelts. The instructions went something like this: "Chop a hole in the ice, put the hook through the smelt's back, drop the smelt into the hole, and when the red flag goes up, pull in the salmon." End of lesson. Obviously, when you're three sheets to the wind, anything sounds easy, so for Mort and Wally, there was no lack of confidence about catching fish. It was just a matter of how many and how big.

With the campfire blazing and six holes cut, baited, and set, my dad and I took to the lake in the Ford like Tunk was a thirty-lane highway. And while learning to drive a car sure excited me, gourmets of the world will be far more interested in learning Wally's recipe for "Tunk Lake Potato Fries." It's quite special:

- Save all the bacon fat from supper
- Save all the bacon fat from breakfast
- Combine the two in a cast-iron frying pan, and attempt to reheat over an open "campfire" in zero weather
- Add chopped onions and a slab of salt pork
- Throw in slices of raw potato
- Serve with blackened hot dogs, cooked on the end of sticks
- Optional: Crows love road kill, so feed it all to them

The two high points of the day were: (a) Bobby pulled in a one-and-a-half-pound togue (that's a lake trout) while Wally was nursing a bad burn from the bacon fat, and (b) I did not strip the gears on the Ford.

Wally insisted on freezing the togue and taking it back to Bangor to show the members of the band. Given the true sportsmen that the band members were, it can be assumed that the fish ended up in the mouth of a saxophone.

Four years later, very close to the spot where my dad

thought I had stripped the gears on the Ford ("Now you've gone and done it!"), my Cousin Keith and I were rowing along the shoreline of Big Tunk trolling two lines, each with a big glob of worms on the end. Suddenly Keith's reel went off, and it was smokin'! He set the line quicker 'n a snap and handed the rod to me. "Keep 'er nice and snug-tight," he said, "I'll handle the net."

This was a big fish. My first really big fish. I was twelve; Keith was fourteen, but he had the wherewithal of a much more mature man. He reeled in the other line while gently coaching me as the action took us slowly around the bend, putting the boat directly in front of the big log home of Admiral Byrd.

At this point, the salmon was breaking the surface about every thirty seconds, and Keith just kept almost whispering to me, "Keep 'er snug . . . keep 'er snug-tight." Then the yelling started. There must have been twenty, thirty guests partying it up on the Byrd house porch.

"Hey, you fellas!" they shouted. "Get out of here! This is private property! Get out of here! Move it out! This is private property!" Three of them then managed to get into a boat and row out toward us, waving and hollering like we were real trespassers. That's also when my world's biggest salmon jumped for the last time, taking with it the leader and all.

"Jack," Keith said sternly (knowing that I could be a real smart-ass), "let me do the talkin'."

After being rudely told that we were in the presence of

Admiral Byrd (one of the three men in the boat) and having our who-did-we-think-we-were rights read to us, Keith spoke up. Our great-grandparents, he explained, once owned the very property the Byrd place sat on. Our family, he went on, had been fishing Tunk Lake for nearly a century. Lastly, and still very politely, he pointed out that Tunk was not a private body of water but one open to all licensed fishermen.

Several days later, someone dropped off a gift for each of us at our homes in West Sullivan, with handwritten notes of apology from Admiral Byrd. No, I didn't keep mine. I was—and still am—just so very, very proud of my Cousin Keith.

Today, my son Johnny and I still travel into Tunk, put up a tent on Sandy Beach, and wet a line in the shadow of Caribou Mountain. Even with the added population of a few camps at that end of Big Tunk, one thing remains the same: "On a clear day you can still read the front page of the *Bangor Daily,* straight down through ten feet of water."

9

A Couple
of Suckers

My mother, Marjie, was a great little woodsman. I say little, because she only stood four feet, ten inches tall and weighed in at about a hundred pounds with her winter coat on. But, the youngest of twenty-one kids, she grew up in Danforth, Maine, down in Washington County, and she knew the woods.

Ever eat a wild mushroom, or did you pass because you thought it might have been a poisonous toadstool? Marjie taught me how to tell the difference, and I can promise you, wild mushrooms are mighty tasty. She also taught me the difference between "pitch" and spruce gum, introduced me to the fresh taste of checkerberry leaves, and showed me how to find fiddlehead greens in the spring.

Two or three times a week, we'd hike off into the woods, which started a seven-iron or so behind our West Sullivan home. Usually we'd take the same route: up past the old graveyard, through a field, into the trees, and down a really steep cliff to the Mill Stream and its man-made dam. It was so old and so far back in the woods that even Marjie was always amazed as to how it got there. Normally we would then follow the flow of the stream back out to the main road and head for home.

This day, though, Ma decided we'd go in the opposite direction, heading upstream to "take a look." And take a look we did. Following the water's flow, we walked through mosquitoes and whipping branches for near a half-hour, then came out onto a wide-open heath. At this point, the stream had dwindled to a brook of about four feet wide and no more than two feet deep. Suddenly, Marjie said, "Look!"

Two giant-size trout were just lolling in the sunny water, facing the current like they had no place to go. Their fins were barely moving, and their tails were just keeping them from slipping downstream.

Earlier, we had broken off a couple of "walking sticks" from some dried alders, and I tried jabbing at the fish. No luck. They just moved under the bank and out of sight.

I could hardly wait to get home and tell Keith.

That summer, he was twelve and I was ten. We had fished the Mill Stream for brookies many times, with angleworms, and had seen a fair amount of success. But I'm talking six-, eight-, ten-inch brookies—not the eighteen-inch giants that Mom and I encountered.

Keith's eyes got about as big as two eyes can get as my outstretched hands described the size of our discovery up on the heath. We doped out a plan: No worms. We would strike out with a fly rod, one that had been gifted to Keith's father, Dwight, from some summer tourists whom Dwight had guided on a very successful fishing trip. It was a Shakespeare that Keith claimed was worth "hundreds and hundreds of dollars." In any event, it was an expensive rod.

Strike out we did, following the same route Marjie and I had taken, straight back to the heath. Once we broke out of the woods, we slowed down to a crawl in order not to spook the trout we hoped would still be there. Then, hearing me exclaim, "Son of a whore!" about three times in rapid succession, Keith turned and saw the snake curled around my leg.

At age ten in West Sullivan, short pants were the normal summer dress. Except for Sunday school. If you wore your Sunday-school pants during the week, the chances were pretty good they'd get caught up in your bike chain, leaving a bunch of greasy little holes around the cuff. And Marjie would get ticked no end.

So here I am in my short pants with a Christless milk adder curled around my leg. I know it's a milk adder, Keith knows it's a milk adder, and we both know this snake's bite can be pretty poisonous. So Keith whips it good with the fly rod—good enough to get it off my bare leg. Then, he opens up his jackknife and, in seconds, that snake is in two pieces. So is the fly rod.

Dwight worked at the Green Front store in Ellsworth, and according to the boys around town "he never touched a drop." Although, on one occasion, when my folks were having company down from Bangor, I did see him sipping on a wine cooler.

It was his habit to arrive home from work every evening at roughly 6:27 or 6:28, give or take a second or two. And on this evening, the seconds seemed like hours. Keith and I were sitting in front of the open barn door, with the mangled fly rod on the ground, when Dwight drove up the driveway.

Tall, dark, and very angular, he had a great laugh when he was so inclined. When he saw the fly rod he was not "so inclined." But Dwight knelt down, picked up and held the pieces of the treasured rod in his hands, and listened to every detail of our "adventure." And, at the end of our story, he stood up, looked down, and said, "Boys, there aren't any trout up in those waters; what you saw were suckers—trash fish."

He gave us both a head pat and walked into the house with the broken fly rod. That was the last word ever spoken about the incident.

❧ 10 ᘑ

Timing—It's Very Important

"G'bottlin'" was really two words pronounced as one: *go bottling.* As in, "Hey, Keith. Wanna' g'bottlin'?" It meant that we'd each take a side of the road, carrying an empty burlap feed bag, and walk along for several miles in search of empty bottles.

This was not just your basic physical endeavor; this was a money-making operation, and there was a science to it. Plus, it required a fair amount of salesmanship.

The science was twofold. First, no matter where you started bottlin', it was critical that you ended up at Emery Dunbar's store in Sullivan Harbor. It was the only place around that sold beer, ergo, the only place where you could cash in your empties or empties that you found. (Emery also took soda pop bottles.) It was the busiest store around, but its unique feature was its location. Location not as in, "Location! Location! Location!" but as in, "the most spectacular view in all of Maine."

You know exactly where it is if you've ever driven Route 1 toward Calais, no more than a few miles east of

Ellsworth. You're driving along through Sullivan Harbor when all of a sudden you look to the right and whammo! there's Frenchman Bay and, eight miles across the water, Cadillac Mountain. Few people can pass this stretch without stopping and being taken in by its sheer beauty. That Emery's little beer store was located precisely in this spot can only be likened to there being a takeout-pizza place on top of Mount Katahdin.

But it was, and that's where bottlin' trips had to end. It was part of the science.

The other part of the science was strategy. In any business, there are good days and bad days. Bottlin's no different. Mondays were generally pretty good. And after a three-day weekend, a Monday, would be considered "el primo." Any Friday—especially after a Thursday night dance at the East Sullivan Grange Hall—would be like following in the tracks of Ding Mills and his beer-drinking buddies, who would chuck "dead soldiers" out of their car windows like they weren't even worth a nickel. Well, most of them wouldn't bring a nickel. But the empty quarts would, and the stubbies were worth a penny. Yup, Fridays were good.

Friday was also "movie night" at the Alhambra in North Sullivan. There were two showings: one at seven, the other about ten minutes after the first one was over. So, if you had made enough money bottlin' during the day, the conversation on the way home from Emery's normally involved anticipation of the movie and, equally important,

"Who you gonna' sit next to?" For me, it was always pretty much Dora Beane.

I'd spot her before the theater lights dimmed and sit two or three seats away. Once the theater got dark, I'd work my way over next to her, which I always felt was pretty crafty. If I had sat down beside her while the lights were on, Gerald Estabrook would have blabbed out, "Havey's sitting next to Dora Beane! Havey's sitting next to Dora Beane!" Eventually that would have gotten back to my mother, and she'd have put in her two cents worth, since Dora was three years older than me. Yup, there were times when you had to be crafty. During one movie, when Shirley Temple's dog was dying, Dora got to sniffing and couldn't stop. So I held her hand. Very crafty!

The other thing Gerald Estabrook loved to do—and this, I thought, was pretty funny—is he'd yell out, "Why did she have to die at the end?" when we'd come out of the theater. This was done expressly for the benefit of all the Summer People, standing in line for the second showing. My mother always thought Gerald was a real stitch.

But, back to the strategy of g'bottlin' for fun and profit. It was also important to think about "timing." If you arrived at Emery Dunbar's store during the noon hour, both Emery and his helper, Phil Woodworth, would be pretty much out straight, causing Emery to ask, "How much you got there, fellas?" We'd tell him, he'd cash us up, and we'd be out of there—bing, bam, boom.

On the other hand, earlier in the morning or later in

the day—when they weren't all that busy—Emery'd tell Phil to cash us up, and that could be a real disaster. As in, "This ain't no good, there's a chip on the neck." Or, "You di'n't get this one here; we don't stock it no more." But generally, after a little salesmanship (read: begging), Emery would chuckle up a smile, shake his head, and pay us in full. Timing—it's very important.

For those who might be thinking about getting into the business, try to avoid "the leak dilemma." For us, an empty quart of Narragansett was a very exciting find—the fastest nickel in the world. But, if there was still a half-inch of stale ale inside that dark brown bottle, the stuff would drain through our burlap bags and get all over our short pants.

Your mother might not like that . . . nickel or no nickel.

❧ 11 ❧

Working Hands

If you've never seen a pair of hands the likes of Bart Joy's, you've missed a vision.

He was the town's blacksmith emeritus, and his shop was at the bottom of the hill leading up the North Sullivan road toward Willie Havey's general store.

Bart's home was about a half-mile down from ours, right there on the main road heading to Sullivan Harbor. It was a nice, big, old, immaculate yellow place that looked down on Preble Cove. Heavily decorated on the outside by wrought-iron creations Bart had forged during earlier years, the house was surrounded by flower gardens.

Mrs. Joy was into the decorative, even in her daily wardrobe, which leaned toward the bright and floral and which won her the title of "Queen Mother" among the observers at the post office. My Grandmother Havey, who never spoke ill of anyone, once commented that Mrs. Joy, "must get out of bed in the morning dressed for a tea up at the Blaine mansion in Augusta." Others, like my mother, were just envious that Mrs. Joy went to her own hairdresser once a week over in Ellsworth.

The Joys owned the only Essex around, and she drove it; Bart always walked. But if they were going someplace special, like to church or on a shopping trip, he would ride—always in the back seat. She'd be up front, at the wheel, and he'd be in the back, reading a copy of *Collier's* or *Liberty,* or just nodding off.

Most frequently though, you would see Bart Joy walking up the main road, more than just a little stooped, heading for the blacksmith shop. There he had spent a lifetime bent over—shoeing horses, forging felling-axes and mattocks, and making wagon-wheel rims and sleigh runners, chains and plows. Yup, he did all that, in addition to keeping the tools of the North Sullivan granite industry in fine working order.

Since Bart had more or less retired, the townfolks weren't exactly lined up to see him, but there were still enough workhorses around to give him a reason to open up and spend a few hours a day in the very special environment of this crusty old blacksmith shop. 'Course, there were two other reasons he went there every day: Mrs. Joy had a very low tolerance of those who smoked and those who drank. Bart did both.

In fact, there were folks around town who claimed that as many as nine or ten pints of Seagrams could be stashed away inside the shop at any given time. Nobody ever accused Bart of having a low tolerance for good whiskey. That would be Mrs. Joy they were thinking about.

There were also those around town who knew of, and marveled at, the spiral-bound notebook that Bart kept in his shop. It was loaded with sketches of devices he had invented in his mind. And these were detailed drawings, with precise measurements and working instructions for things he knew he could build. The actual construction may have never happened, but that didn't matter.

I never forgot what he told me on a hot afternoon when we were sitting together out front. I was ten. Bart was whittling on a piece of pine, and I asked him, "What are you making?"

He said, "I don't know. But when my hands are working, my mind comes up with some pretty great ideas."

The blacksmith shop was a stand-alone building that sat twenty or thirty feet back from the road. The entrance was guarded by barn-type sliding doors, secured with a special double-locking system that Bart himself had concocted. Once those doors were opened, the daylight would reveal a single, scruffy room filled with history: the anvil, the forge, the lengths of long-worn leather harnesses, the coal box, the stacks of outdated magazines, the water tank, and a myriad of working tools long past their prime.

Every year since he opened his shop, Bart had nailed one horseshoe to the big beam that ran end-to-end inside the building. There were forty-nine of them— a declaration of forty-nine years of hard work, not necessarily accomplished without the benefit of fine Cuban cigars and a slight buzz.

Then there was the long wooden bench.

This was a true piece of work. Names, initials, and dates going back to the 1800s were carved in the smoothed-down, aged wood, attesting to its many occupants. Bart could recall a story relating to each. Every day, having opened up the shop, he would pull the long wooden bench out into the sunshine, pick up the remains of the half-smoked, half-chewed cigar he had left on the anvil the day before, sit down on the bench, and light up.

But once he got his stogie going to perfection, Bart would step back into the shop, put on his leather apron, and stoke up the coal-fired furnace 'til the sizzle of the spit on his thumb against a pair of red-hot tongs told him the heat was ready for forging iron. During a normal week, six and maybe eight good horses would go back to work with new shoes. Once in a while, Bart would shoe the town's one and only riding horse, which was owned by Buddy Blaisdell.

Buddy was a handsome cut of a man, single and in his late twenties. He was a salesman for some big company, and according to Shirley Clemmons, when Buddy was away he stayed at some of the fanciest hotels in New York and Boston.

Back home, he wore real riding britches and tall, shiny boots, and he slicked his hair straight back with Wildroot. At least, my mother said it was Wildroot, and having

Bart Joy used to get onto Buddy Blaisdell something fierce.

worked at Ligette's Drugstore in Bangor for two years before she and my dad were married, she was in a position to know.

Bart Joy used to get onto Buddy Blaisdell something fierce—all because Buddy used to show off big-time and ride his pinto pony, called Geronimo, straight down the main road, whooping it up and racing locals who were driving their cars or trucks. Now, pavement can be pretty hard on a horse's hoofs, and Buddy knew it. Bart used to caution him, but Buddy'd bring the pinto in to be shod and claim he never rode on tarred roads. On one occasion, Bart picked up a red-hot shoe in his iron tongs, held it very, very close to Buddy Blaisdell's nose, and asked, "Do I look like a rookie?"

Yup, that Buddy was a showman, which is why he accepted Bobby Black's challenge for the Sunday when the Sullivan men's baseball team was scheduled up to play the Steuben Athletic Club, right there on the ballfield across from our house. Bobby bragged that he could take Buddy in a twenty-lap race around the bases—Bobby on his '36 Harley, Buddy on his pinto.

According to Stubby Scott, who took tickets at the Alhambra and was also the catcher for the Sullivan team, "Never again will you see a sight like that."

The home-team bleachers were built to hold thirty people, more than enough for a normal Sunday game. The away team had a bench for a dozen players and a second one for six or eight "family members and friends."

Would you believe that on that day, cars were lined up
on both sides of the main road, as far as you could count?
Friends of my folks had long since filled our driveway,
and some had parked on the lawn. Ding Mills was out
like a light under Aunt Zelda's shade tree, an hour before
the race was scheduled to start. This was going to be
B . . . I . . . G!

Maybe because he was captain of the men's baseball
team, Stubby got to be the designated starter for the race,
and promptly at noon he instructed "the boys" to take
their positions behind home plate. "Twenty laps. May the
best man win!"

When the contestants rounded third base on the first
lap, Bobby swung wide on his Harley, ran into a batch of
loose gravel, and slid thirty feet into the Quaker State Oil
sign. The siren of the ambulance from Hancock added a
new dimension to the event. Bobby took twenty stitches in
his left arm and a cast on his left leg. The Harley suffered
but a few scratches.

Buddy and Geronimo were declared the winners. The
spectators, who had been anticipating a long and grueling
event, recalled the Joe Louis–Max Schmeling heavyweight
championship boxing match, when Louis knocked out the
Nazi German in 124 seconds.

I remember it like it was yesterday.

❦ 12 ❧

Painters and Porcupines

Satan and I were born at the same time or, at least, during the same year. And for a decade we were the closest of friends. He was a coal black German shepherd with straight-up, pointed ears and a smiling tail. Where I went—on bike or on foot—he went, too. The reverse was not always true.

This otherwise incredibly smart animal had a propensity for chasing down porcupines. And he'd do it repeatedly—a habit that did not draw the affections of my Uncle Dwight.

"Where's Satan, Ma?" I would ask.

"He's out in the shed, waiting for your Uncle Dwight to come home from work."

Having gotten the call from my mother, Dwight would arrive home from the Green Front in Ellsworth, down his supper, then head across the path to our place with a pair of pliers. He'd go to the shed, drag Satan into the kitchen by the collar, and examine the damage. A coal black dog (or a white one) that gets a snout full of porcupine is not a pretty sight. The quills are all over its face, inside its nostrils, in the roof of its mouth, in its lips, and stuck in its eyelids.

Knowing the drill, Satan would hug the floor and take on the most sheepish of looks. But what had to be had to be, and he knew it. Dwight was a master of the art—always knowing when to be mean and tough, always knowing when to talk sympathetically to the pup.

For the uninitiated, porcupine quills are not like needles with straight points. They're more like fishhooks with barbs. So the removal process is difficult and extremely painful. And bloody. Dwight would spread newspapers all over the kitchen floor, close the dining room door, and start with the easy ones. I'd go in the dining room and turn up the radio to drown out the howling. Later that night, Satan would come up and fall asleep at the foot of my bed, damn glad it was over.

Even though this dog looked like a ferocious black wolf, he was gentle as a lamb. He never growled. He only barked when we were playing on the beach or on the lawn. The townfolks loved him. Strangers, on the other hand, weren't easily convinced that he wasn't an attack dog.

Take the morning Satan and I were over at Jimmy Dickens's garage.

Ding Mills was pumping gas into a shiny, new, black Buick driven by Summer People. He looked down, saw Satan, grabbed him around the neck and rolled to the ground, yelling to anyone around, "Help! Save me! Save me!"

The windows in that Buick went up quicker than greased lighting. I'm sure those folks from away never saw my dog licking Ding's face.

Then there was Waldo Peirce, the internationally known artist whose paintings hung in the collections of the wealthy from Paris to New York, including Franklin Delano Roosevelt, Paulette Goddard, and Burgess Meredith.

During the late thirties, this giant of a man, with his giant red beard and his giant talent, was a frequent visitor to our home in West Sullivan. On weekends, when my father was home, there'd be a whole gang in, singing it up around the piano 'til the wee hours of the morning. But Waldo would also stop by on weekdays, when my old man wasn't home.

On those occasions, Marjie would get all spiffed up in something she had made—like a pretty bandanna skirt with a white top, and scrubbed white sneakers. Whether this guy ever put a hit on my mother or not, I don't know. I was too young to know. But I was aware that she liked the attention—well-deserved attention that she wasn't getting from my dad.

And I know something else for sure: Satan did not like Waldo Peirce.

He liked Ding Mills. He liked Albert Jewett's two cows. He liked our cat, Jigger, who would snuggle up against him and go to sleep. But he did not like porcupines, and he did not like the artist Waldo Peirce.

When Waldo drove into our yard in his Model-T Ford Banana Wagon, which was always filled with tubes of oil paint, brushes, and stretched canvases, Satan acted like a different dog. He would start barking at the sight of the car as it came up the drive; when the Ford pulled to a stop, the dog would stand back from the driver's side door and go into his growl mode, which I had rarely ever seen.

Then, during the time that my mother and Waldo would sit out on the front lawn sipping iced tea, Satan would lie on the ground, about twelve feet away. And he wouldn't budge—unless Waldo moved. If the painter stood up, Satan stood up. On an occasion that I recall vividly, Waldo rose and extended his massive hand to pat Sate on the nose. Bad move. Satan's ears slicked back, and his upper lip curled, showing his brilliant white teeth—including a good-sized fang on each side. The dog's growl was hardly perceivable.

That was the end of Waldo's attempts at petting. He excused himself to our outhouse in the shed and wisely saved his right hand for more famous works.

Dogs. You just never know.

❧ 13 ❧

The Sporting Thing

In a town where spectator events were rare, Sullivan team baseball was pretty exciting stuff.

You could always tell when "the opener" was coming up because Henry Bunker would ride over the bridge from Hancock with his horses and mowing machine, and do the entire outfield. That didn't make it look like Fenway Park, but the grass was pretty special by the time he finished up. It was an exciting event.

Especially for me, with the ballfield right across the road from our house and with the knowledge that Eddy Crosby would be at each game with his wagon, selling steamed hot dogs and soda pop. Of course, just before game time he'd have to "close her down," because he was the town team's shortstop. And, he wouldn't be there during the seventh-inning stretch, because that's when the whole team went to Bobby Black's Garage for cold sodas.

Even before I saw Henry Bunker and his horses, I could always tell that the opening game was about to happen, because Uncle Dwight would start warming up his curveball—his split-fingered curveball, to be more exact. Dwight was the starting pitcher for the Sullivan town team. In fact, he was its only pitcher.

Likewise, Stubby Scott, the team's captain, was the one and only catcher. Once he got into his entire outfit—chest protector, shin guards, and mask—his five-foot, two-hundred-pound frame was truly a sight to behold. But Stubby, one of the great jokesters in town, easily laughed off comments relating to his "baby gorilla" figure. Plus, he was fearless behind the plate.

My Cousin Keith and I played being Stubby during Dwight's "spring training" workouts, which normally took place the week before the Fourth of July. We didn't own a catcher's mitt, but we had one outfielder's glove, and in the evenings, we'd take turns catching Dwight's infamous curveball, out in the driveway after he got home from the Green Front.

My uncle would toss a string of soft, straight pitches to each of us. Then, once his arm got loosened up, he'd pull the trigger on the curve. Just to catch this pitch was a feat in itself; to hit it required a talent that few opposition players down east possessed. Once he got it working, Dwight would take his curve to the next level: He'd cup the ball in his glove, bring it up in front of his face, then treat it to a little fresh spit. Now, if you think his basic curve was a hummer, you should've seen it with spit and all. Trying to hit that mother was enough to throw a grown man out of joint!

But, defeating just any grown man was not the challenge for the Sullivan players. The summer opener was a home game against the Milbridge town team. That was the challenge!

They said the animosity between Sullivan and Milbridge started back in the mid-twenties, when Oral "Swisher" Whalen was playing on the Sullivan High basketball team. The controversial game, as many still remembered, was played at the Milbridge Town Hall, which was heated by a woodstove at one end of the court.

The score of that particular contest was all tied in the last period, when Oral drove to the basket for an easy layup. In mid-stride, he got a full body block from two Milbridge players and went flying into the stove. Well, that was always a risk, and plenty of players got burned on that old stove. The thing that ticked everyone off (everyone from Sullivan, that is) was that when Oral hit the woodstove his glasses fell off, and one of the Milbridge fans flung 'em into the crowd. That was the end of the game for Oral, and Sullivan High lost by two.

So, our upcoming summer-baseball opener against Milbridge was, as always, the continuation of a time-honored, rip-snorting grudge match. Game time was three o'clock on the Fourth, and cars started lining up along the main road, which bordered the first-base line, shortly after high noon. From there, the early-comers would be able to sit on the roofs of their vehicles and enjoy the best seats in the house, so to speak.

Besides, the Milbridge team would arrive first for batting practice, and everyone wanted to be in position to extend an appropriate "welcome" to the enemy, in addition to lashing out with a few choice catcalls at "Tank" Tapley, the so-called "impartial" umpire from Franklin. According to Stubby, Tank couldn't organize "a two-car funeral," never mind take charge of a nine-inning ball game. But he was the only "local" who'd do it—on that both teams could agree.

The day was hot, and the blackflies were having their own field-day celebration. At the end of the sixth inning, Sullivan was leading two-zip, thanks to Carl Gray's bases-loaded double. Dwight went to the mound in the top of the seventh and put the visitors down one-two-three.

All hell didn't break loose until the long-awaited seventh-inning stretch.

First, Emery Dunbar came up from his store toting a barrel filled with iced-down bottles of Pickwick Ale for the Sullivan players.

On the other side of the field, members of the Milbridge team broke out their own keg of something they said made "homemade hand grenades." They dared Ding Mills to chug-a-lug a paper cup full, and he did. The next morning he claimed it was strong enough to kick a rutting bull moose all the way to Hancock Point.

When it came time for him to announce that the seventh-inning stretch had stretched out long enough, umpire Tank Tapley was yelling for the teams to "Play

During the seventh-inning stretch, the whole team went to Bobby Black's Garage for cold sodas.

ball!" But the only ones listening were the local kids, who were all over the ball field, making like they were Ted Williams, Dom DiMaggio, or Jimmy "Double X" Foxx.

That was about the time Aunt Zelda came rushing across the main road to tell Dwight that their hog had broken out of the pen. This was a very big deal. I mean, the pig was on his way to four hundred pounds, and folks don't like to see their winter bacon running around exercising on a hot summer's day. Plus, this was a mean hog.

Normally, when he broke out, the hog would just go into the garden and ruin a few rows of peas or corn. But on this day, Dwight's two dogs—Duke and Nina— decided to give chase. They ran that hog all the way to Bart Joy's front lawn and drove it straight into Mrs. Joy's petunia patch, planted neatly in a used, white-walled tire off their Essex. By the time Dwight arrived, Mrs. Joy was whaling the pure living hell out of that hog with a house broom, all the while yelling, "Bart, get your gun and do something!"

Well, you don't lead a horse to water, and you darn sure don't lead a four-hundred pound hog back to his pen. But with the help of two zillion school kids, who quickly transformed themselves from baseball stars into Teddy Roosevelt's Rough Riders, Dwight managed. He also managed to pick up a wicked gash on the palm of his right hand while wrassling the hog into the dilapidated pigpen.

But Dwight wasn't the only casualty of the day.

Over on the ball field, Milbridge's Duncan Porter was out in center field—as in, "out cold" in center field. Moreover, the attitude of Duncan's teammates was not exactly sympathetic. "Duncan," they declared, "can stay there 'til Labor Day, for all he's worth!"

Tank Tapley said there was nothing in his umpire's rule book to cover this kind of situation, so he declared that the game would continue. But after Sullivan poked five unchallenged hits into center field, running the score up to six–zip in the eighth with no outs, he changed his mind and pronounced Sullivan the winner.

As the sun was going down, Stubby Scott and Eddy Crosby were about to leave when they remembered poor Duncan still lying in center field. So they drove Eddy's wagon out there, poured Duncan into the back, and drove him home to Milbridge.

Stubby said, "It was the only sporting thing to do."

❧ 14 ❧

Death Before
Dishonor

Randall "Itchie" Taylor's barber shop was two
buildings up the road from the North Sullivan post office,
and he was really the only honest-to-goodness barber
around. His nickname highlighted the fact that he was
always scratching himself, like an animal with fleas.

Inside, the shop was a long, narrow affair with maybe
ten or so seats for waiting customers and two, pearl white
barber chairs. (Itchie always said he was fixing to hire a
second barber, but he never did.) In front of the two big
chairs was an oilcloth-covered shelf that displayed an
array of hair oils and creams that gave the place its own
special scent.

The town had its amateur hair cutters, like my
mother, who thought that because they had a comb and a
pair of scissors they could do the "barbering" of family
members, but that would be stretching it for sure. One
look in the mirror after Marjie cut my hair, and I knew it
would be weeks before my head would be back to normal.
Yet, whenever she gave me the twenty-five cents it cost to

go up to Taylor's barber shop she would later be extremely critical of Itchie's work, as in, "Doesn't he know that you part your hair on the right side?"

In any event, Itchie—not Marjie—owned the one and only official, red-white-and-blue barber pole in town. So, it was to Taylor's that most of the men in town went for a shave or a haircut or both.

Itchie only opened up on Thursdays, Fridays, and Saturdays; the rest of the week he dug wells. And according to Buzz Burrell, a former selectman, Itchie was "the best you could get" if you needed a well dug. But his talents didn't stop there. The town barber was a world of information on statistics—sports statistics. I mean, he could tell you flat out, how many singles, doubles, triples, and home runs the Splendid Splinter had during his first year up with the Red Sox. And how many times Williams struck out.

Lou Finney, Jim Tabor, Pete Fox, Bobby Dorr? Itchie had all the numbers on all the players. In fact, the centerpiece of his tiny barber shop was a crackly old Zenith radio that never moved off WLBZ, which carried the voice of the Red Sox, Jim Britt. In the summer, you'd walk in for a haircut and think there were ten or eleven people in line ahead of you. In truth, there were only two. The rest were just hanging out listening to the game and taking in all of Itchie Taylor's insider expertise.

In addition to an amazing memory, Itchie had a cat, a three-legged stray named Tripod, that would want

Itchie Taylor owned the one and only official,
red-white-and-blue barber pole in town.

to come in . . . go out . . . come in . . . go out . . . come in . . . go out—easily three or four times during a single haircut. And with every entrance and exit, the shop's screen door would screek like a piece of chalk running over a blackboard. The boys playing cribbage would take the distraction with a, "Think that door needs a little oil, Itch?" But they seemed to prefer musing about it than taking any action, so the door kept squeaking.

Unlike the West Sullivan post office, Taylor's Barber Shop was more a forum for sports and politics than the breezy, who's-doing-what-to-whom type of gossip you'd pick up at the other end of town. Plus, Itchie's place was totally a "man's world"—Cora Woodman being the exception. They used to say that Cora never let her husband, Woody, out of her sight, even when he needed a haircut. She'd come waltzing through the squeaking screen door with poor, old Woody in tow, see that all the waiting seats were occupied, turn in disgust, and whine, "Come on, Woodman. I'm taking you to the barber in Ellsworth!" Then she'd bang out the door.

Cora would carry on the same way for two, maybe three days in a row 'til she hit it right and landed Woody a decent place in line. Once seated, she'd start in—first, on Itchie. As in, "When are you getting rid of that sick cat?" Then she'd turn on Woody, "Sit up in your seat, Woodman! You're slumped over like an old man." Then it would be, "What is that stinking smell in here?" (It was the dried cod strips the boys would always pull out of a brown paper bag, pass around, and eat in honor of Cora's presence.)

My mother claimed that when Cora was younger and first started dating Woody, she used to be the life of the party. Not only would she arm-wrestle the boys down at Bobby Black's garage, she'd ride on the back of Bobby's Harley, "going like sixty straight up the North Sullivan Road." But then she caught menopause "at a very early age" and commenced to get real bitchy.

It wore on Woody, and when she wasn't around he'd always talk about leaving town and joining the U.S. Navy. But the closest he ever got to that was taking a Saturday night trip to Bangor and getting tattooed down on Hancock Street. The design was a blue-and-red skull and crossbones, along with the words "Death Before Dishonor" inscribed on a scroll. Somehow, it just never quite seemed to fit Woody's personality.

When asked about this body decoration, Cora would say, "He should have had a chicken tattooed on his ass, along with the word 'loser.' "

❧ 15 ❧

Hangin' Out
in Bangor

Statistics prove
Near and far
That folks who drive
Like crazy
Are!

Mort Havey's '36 Ford coupe could cover the forty-nine miles from West Sullivan to downtown Bangor in about sixty-five minutes, depending on the traffic in Ellsworth shortly after six o'clock on any given morning.

During the summer months, my father traveled back and forth to work every day, and on occasions, I'd ride along with him and go visit my Aunt Louise and Cousin Bob (son of the Tunk Lake chef). Or I'd hang out at my Aunt Dora Malkson's millinery shop on Central Street, where she designed and fashioned women's hats for the well-to-do. (As a result, she became pretty well-to-do herself.) Aunt Dora was my mother's oldest sister and was, in fact, old enough to be Ma's mother.

It was generally cool and foggy when we shot out of our West Sullivan driveway, and Marjie would always make me wear a sweater until the car heater got warm—like, by the time we reached Ellsworth Falls. Once we got past that point, garbled voices or music would attempt to cut through the static on the Ford's Philco radio, and Mort would start spinning the dial in an effort to pick up the morning news. Maybe it had something to do with his being a newsman by profession, but he could dial-spin that Philco quicker 'n it was ever built to be spun.

When we reached Bangor, the city would be just beginning to wake up, so I'd follow Mort up the creaky, oily stairs to the *Commercial* newsroom on Main Street, find an empty chair, and sleep 'til I dared to call someone on the phone. Aunt Louise, who normally accompanied Wally's band while they did their nightly gigs at the Roseland Ballroom, did not appreciate having her phone ring before sunrise. Quick study that I was, I knew better than to put her otherwise pleasant personality to the test.

Chubby McPhee would be at his Underwood tattooing a sheet of paper with a story for the sports page of the *Commercial*'s afternoon edition at a rate of speed in excess of what two fingers can normally accomplish on a typewriter. The only thing faster in his dingy corner of the already dingy newsroom office was the rate of speed this one-eyed sportswriter snuffed out one Kool after another in a dingy, overfilled ashtray.

Chub's glass eye never slowed his excitement and enthusiasm for anything related to sports—particularly the teams of John Bapst High, from which he had recently graduated. Moreover, it wasn't that easy to tell which of his eyes was the real one, since his everyday glasses had last been cleaned God only knows when.

Elizabeth "Beth" Schoppee, the paper's society writer, would sit at her phone, just inches away from Chub's desk, gabbing about a soon-to-take-place charity dance at the Penobscot Country Club.

Her bright red lipstick and Boston-bought fashions suggested a leap or two beyond the reality of the unkempt surroundings, and her perfume stank up Chub's space like something from outer space. Decked out in high heels every day, Beth might have acquired her stiff-legged walk in order not to lose her balance on the uneven newsroom floor, but I always thought she walked stiff-legged everywhere.

And that wasn't all. After her finishing-school days, she had spent enough time in Boston and on Cape Cod to conjure up her own version of a New England accent, and it wasn't like anything you'd hear down east!

The only thing that could compete with the smell of Beth's icky perfume came from the next desk over and the sickly sweet Rum & Maple tobacco smoke billowing out of Don Daley's freshly lit pipe. He'd puff nonstop as he attempted to gather facts from the Bangor Police Department in regard to a minor theft of milk "in broad daylight" from a doubled-parked Grant's truck on outer Hammond Street.

In case his suspenders ever gave out, Don always wore a belt as a backup. And he always carried a lot of change in his pocket, so if I begged him long enough he'd take me across the corner to Frawley's Drug Store and buy me a strawberry ice-cream soda. That just happened to be the best strawberry ice-cream soda in the whole cotton pickin' world, and you don't have to take my word for it. Lots of folks thought so.

Six other desks—all stacked with papers, folders, binders, and other stuff—filled the rest of the city room. One was occupied by Lincoln "Please-don't-call-me-Linc!" Dunbar, the bow tie-wearing writer of the paper's editorials. It was said that he allowed his wife, Francine, to make all "minor" decisions. As in, where to send the kids to college, what color to paint the house, and where to spend the family's annual vacation. Lincoln, on the other hand, grappled with the major stuff: Should Finland declare war against the Russians? Where should the next World's Fair be held? On which bridges and highways should Maine taxpayers' money be spent? Lincoln had definite opinions on all these weighty issues.

New Dartmouth grad Bill McKenna sat gripping the edge of yet another city-room desk while awaiting word that he would be transferred to the advertising department. Nearby was the loquacious, ever-funny Bud Leavitt, who was destined to become famous as the outdoor writer for a competing newspaper, the *Bangor Daily News.* Bud dominated the room with a voice so booming it would flush the pigeons off the roof.

And let us not forget the quiet man, Dartmouth alum Ky Ayoob, who would one day become Bud Leavitt's boss at that same competing newspaper.

Yet another new Dartmouth grad, Jack McKernan, was rapidly breaking in as sports editor at the *Commercial.* The future father of a future Maine governor, Jack was the tallest man in the room, measuring nearly six foot seven in his stocking feet. He mostly wore huge (size 13 ½) wingtip brogues, and on those occasions when Mort allowed me to visit the "office," Jack would let me stand on his shoes while he held my hands and walked me around the city room. He was great fun.

The point desk was occupied by B. Morton Havey himself, city editor of this money-losing evening newspaper.

Rounding out the second floor was a glassed-in room with a long wooden table, where a bevy of proofreaders would sit during the late-morning hours, attempting to figure out what the staff writers were trying to spell and where the hell they had learned their grammar. If they missed a beat and a mistake ended up in print, the very meticulous city editor would get very pissed off. I know, because I would have to ride all the way back to West Sullivan with him at the end of the day.

Everyone and his brother knew lantern-jawed George

Mulherrin, who held the fort on the next floor down. His domain was the room with the forever-on red light, where he developed the film he had shot during the day and printed the black-and-white photos that would appear on the pages of the *Bangor Commercial* that evening: car collisions; snow scenes; the funny, the sad, the bad. George had a special touch with his 4 x 5 camera, capturing people, places, and trains with equal skill. He especially liked locomotives. Sometimes he'd let me ride with him on assignment and hold the bag with the film packs.

He used to drive faster 'n a bat out of hell, and why not? All the cops knew him, and if they ever needed tickets for any event in town ol' George would always come up with the necessary freebies—along with one-liners that would knock you out.

Then there was Scotty (I never knew his last name). He worked on the same floor but out at the front of the building, where the presses roared into gear six days a week. Scotty was head pressman, head machinist, and overseer of every dirty, greasy piece of equipment that had to work right in order to get the paper out on the street each day in a timely fashion. Even when it was fifteen below outside, Scotty would take a smoke break by the front door, which looked across Main Street to Freeses Department Store.

The sweat would be rolling down his face over major layers of grease, and he'd be stripped down to his blackened undershirt, also wet with sweat. Scotty's cigarette would burn all the way down to his greasy fingertips. "Hey there redhead," he'd say to me, "how's things down there in Sullivan?" Then we'd talk, and he would tell me stories about growing up in Scotland. He generally ended these conversations with a "Say hi to the ol' man for me," whereupon he'd be back at it.

As different as all these dedicated overachievers were, they found common cause in a single challenge—to beat out the evil forces that sat behind shiny, clean plate-glass windows down on Exchange Street. The enemy was known as the *Bangor Daily News,* the morning paper with the big-name writers and the big-time circulation. Everyone read the *News,* whose circulation stretched well beyond Bangor's city limits. It was even popular in West Sullivan, God forbid.

Unfortunately for Mort and the others, if you asked most folks about the *Bangor Commercial,* the best you got was a "Huh?"

❧ 16 ❧
Food for Thought

My Ma and my Uncle Hal were the youngest of twenty-one Malkson children born down in Danforth, which is in Washington County. In fact, when they were both still toddlers, most of their brothers and sisters had grown up and moved away from home.

In many ways Hal and Marjie were a lot alike. They were both small—about five feet tall. They both had smooth, silky-soft skin. They both had smiling twinkles in their eyes. And they were both artistically creative. The big difference was that Marjie made fast decisions and moved quick as a bee. Hal was the exact opposite. But he had a very lucrative job in Boston, as the interior designer for the Jordan Marsh men's store, and he'd drive his family up to West Sullivan every summer for a week's vacation.

They always arrived on a Saturday afternoon and always in a new green Hudson. Uncle Hal liked green— as did his wife, Mildred; his mother-in-law, Mrs. Bastion; and my Cousin Gloria, who was a little older than me and had a beautiful mezzo soprano voice. Two or three times during the week when they were visiting, we'd all hop into the "Green Hornet" (my name for the Hudson), and Uncle Hal would take her straight to someplace like Gouldsboro and Jimmy Hall's lobster pound, right there on Wonsqueak Harbor.

Uncle Hal and the Hall brothers remembered each other from "the good old days," so they'd dicker a bit over price 'til we had a couple of cardboard boxes chock full of clams and lobsters in the trunk of the Hornet. Then we'd strike out for the big surf down at Schoodic Point and have a great family picnic.

We all loved those lobster bakes, but according to Uncle Hal, they didn't compare to the Saturday night feast my mother always had ready for him on the first evening of the family's arrival from Boston: "Little Marjie Havey's World Famous Saturday Night Salt Pork and Baked Bean Supper," he called it.

First though, it's only fitting that I eat a little crow here, having mouthed off as many times as I have over the years about Ma's less than picture-book cooking. They say that every boy between two and eight owes his mother at least 4,820 apologies. Well, I'm a long way from being caught up on those numbers, but today I'm unleashin' one ol' pounder of an apology to Ma about her cooking. Because Uncle Hal was right. Just one whiff of Marjie's pork and beans was enough to make a dying man rise from his bed and get in line for one last mouthful of her soul-perfected recipe.

*We'd strike out for the big surf down at Schoodic Point
and have a great family picnic.*

But the competition for the "best-in-the-world baked beans" was plenty stiff down east, and I don't mean just in West Sullivan. Consider that everyone from Molasses Pond to Calais ate baked beans for supper every Saturday night. Some of 'em were more than decent, and some of 'em were just halfway decent. But most of 'em were pretty tasty, especially when you were good and hungry. One thing is for sure: There'd be shock at the dinner table on Saturday night if someone came up with a slight change in her baked-bean recipe for the first time in nine or ten generations. I mean, the chance that Arthur Bunker would say to his wife, Mable, at suppertime, "Did you use more brown sugar on these than normal?" was no chance at all.

Lots of the ladies had little secret baking "wrinkles" that they used over the years, but for the most part things were pretty much constant from house to house and family to family. Which explains why nobody ever got too surprised at your basic Grange Hall supper.

Of course, one major taste difference would be the type of bean selected (like red kidney or yellow-eyed or Jacob's cattle or California pea). Such decisions had been made by someone in the family during the Stone Age, never to be varied through the years.

Ma's lifetime choice was the small, dried California pea beans, which she would cover with cold water on Friday and soak overnight. The next morning she'd drain 'em off, add less than a third of a cup of molasses, and put in some Coleman's dry mustard, a touch of brown sugar, and a pinch of black pepper. Next, she'd pour boiling hot water up to the top of the beans, stir 'em all up, then add that all-important half-pound or so of salt pork, which she'd cook separately for a minute or two before layering the strips across the top of the beans. Finally, Marjie would cover the whole kit 'n caboodle and let 'em go for about eight hours in the ol' woodstove oven at, say, 275°. It was during the ninth hour that things started to get tricky. Then, Ma would uncover the pot for good and keep adding a splash of water about every ten minutes 'til her face took on the color of a boiled lobster.

If it happened to be the third Saturday in June, that would be about the time my Uncle Hal would be cresting the hill in Hancock and getting his first look of the year at the Taunton River, the Singing Bridge, and the side-by-side Havey houses over in Sullivan along Route 1. In the back seat of the Hudson would be Mrs. Bastion and my cousin Gloria. Way in back, in the trunk, would be enough luggage for a week's vacation. Up front, riding next to Hal, would be his beautiful wife, my Aunt Mildred.

Hal swore that when he topped that hill—even if the wind was at his back—he could smell the aroma of his little sister's baked beans drifting all the way across the river from West Sullivan.

This was also about the time my dad would be running around sweating in his undershirt as he worked to finish mowing and clipping the lawn—so the place looked halfway decent for the Malksons. He was even known to duck into the pantry for a second and take one quick downer of straight Paul Jones. Because Mort knew one thing for sure: As much as he adored his in-laws, once they arrived nothing would happen quickly. According to my father, standing and watching Uncle Hal make a whiskey sour for Aunt Mil, then a martini for himself, was like watching all of *Gone With the Wind* in slow motion. Twice!

Gerald Estabrook was just startin' to get the hang of smokin' cigarettes when I told him how long it took my Uncle Hal just to light one up. He was dying to watch, and as I kept explaining how Hal would go about it, Gerald kept sayin', "No shit! No shit!" So I finally told him that if he'd keep his big mouth shut, I'd call him down the next morning while Uncle Hal was having a cup of coffee and his first smoke of the day, out by the barn door. That way, I said, he could watch how the city guys did it.

If anyone expected Hal to walk out onto the driveway at nine or so in the morning with a two-day growth, looking like he was on a vacation or something, they had another big thing coming. This was always a dapper fellow—always. He'd have smoothed-back hair, neatly pressed slacks, a nice shirt and sport jacket, a touch of Mennen cologne, and—in the summer—two-tone leather shoes, normally white and brown with pointed toes.

Hal laughed and chatted it up with us while we sat there in admiration—him sipping his coffee, us sitting there on our bikes—until he made the first move for that

*He took one humongous drag, tilted his head back,
then slowly—and I mean slowly—let the smoke
float out from between his lips.*

pack of Luckies inside his sport-jacket pocket.

Gerald nudged me, thinking something was gonna happen. But, Hal was never that fast. Ever. After a while, maybe ten or fifteen minutes, he tapped that pack on the back of his hand until a cigarette slid out, and he rolled it between his thumb and forefinger for five minutes or so. Then he rolled it some more . . . and stopped. He took out his lighter, blew on it a few times, held it for a minute or two . . . then remembered that he wanted to show us something in the trunk of his car. Finally, once he got the Lucky lit, he took one humongus drag, tilted his head back, watched the sky for a bit, then slowly—and I mean very slowly—let the smoke float out from between his lips and watched it curl upward. I heard Gerald Estabrook say under his breath, "Jeezus, I don't believe it."

Soon afterward, on the morning after the Malkson clan left, me and Gerald, and Ma were sitting there in the kitchen, jawin' it up when Gerald asked, "How long will it take Uncle Hal to drive back to Boston?" We just sort of looked at each other.

Good question.

❦ 17 ❦

Hat Shops and Whorehouses

Aunt Dora's millinery shop was right there at 73 Central Street, one story above the Kenduskeag Stream, which flowed merrily through a section of Bangor's business district. At Christmastime she was always the one who took me out to Bronsen's for dinner, then over to Freeses to see you-know-who with the phony beard and red suit. (Believing in Santa is a bit of a stretch once you hit age seven.)

As I've said, my very talented Aunt Dora Malkson created and fashioned ladies hats for those who had the bucks. Which always prompted one of my mother's favorite lines: "I could feed a family of four for a week on what Dora gets for one of those silly hats." That's not to say that Ma wasn't very lovingly attached to my Aunt Dora or that my Aunt Dora wasn't very fond of me, in her old-maid way. She was, but if I bounced into her shop with Satan and she happened to be doing a "fitting" with a customer, it would be, "Out back, Jackie! Out back! And please leave the dog outside!" Maybe Sate understood better than me her overreaction to our "dropping by" because he always seemed relieved to go out and lie next to the building on the sidewalk.

For me, going "out back" in the shop was like journeying into the unknown. It was a huge, dimly lit space filled with fabrics, needles, pins, feathers, buttons, bows, and mousetraps. (Being right there on the Kenduskeag, Aunt Dora's place was home to more than just a few rodents, and I'm not just talking mice here, fellow trappers.) Then there were the hats themselves: some finished, some half-finished, some just started. They were all spread out on a big, round table next to the Singer sewing machine. Beside the Singer was Aunty's upright Chickering piano, which was loaded down with the sheet music for songs like "When the Moon Comes Over the Mountain." (No wonder Sate liked it out on the sidewalk.) But once I got out back I was committed—and obliged to be very, very quiet. I had to wait 'til the "fitting" was over and the customer left. Then Aunt Dora would come give me a big perfumed hug that would mix nicely with the already established backroom aroma of cinnamon incense.

Although, as I said, "I had to wait it out," I could always get her attention if I used the bathroom. Because after the toilet was flushed, the water would keep running until the handle was shaken, and I would keep shaking it real hard until Aunt Dora'd whip out and just glare at me with her hands on her hips. "Going to the bathroom," I would say sweetly, and she'd just look up at God and sigh.

My mother always said, "I could feed a family of four for a week on what Dora gets for one of those silly hats."

On one occasion, when the boredom got especially unbearable during a hat fitting, I opted to practice "Chopsticks" on the Chickering—with the ol' base pedal pressed straight to the floor. Somehow Marjie later caught wind of that event, and I caught pure, livin' hell.

That might have been the same day that I sneaked out of The Women's Hat Shop with two pieces of Aunt Dora's unused cinnamon incense. All the way back to West Sullivan, Mort kept asking, "What the hell did Dora feed you for lunch?" Even though I had the incense wrapped in toilet paper and stuffed deep in my pocket, it still had quite a whiff to it. And it was going to have even more of a whiff if I could get it stashed away in the right place at the post office and persuade one of the boys to light it up.

Junior Bunker always carried matches, and he thought it was a helluva idea. So we stuck the incense behind the Nabisco cookie display, and he lit both pieces while Audrey and Shirley were sortin' the mail. By the time Phil Woodworth came in—followed by telephone operator, Phyllis Havey (no relation)—the whole room was smelling pretty raunchy. "Like a Chinese whorehouse!" according to Phyllis. "Either that or Audrey must have bought some of that "Evening In Paris" stuff from Monkey Wards to go along with her new underwear."

Working as she did for Bell Tel, Phyllis always seemed to know what other people were talking about.

❧ 18 ❧

The Man Who Hardly Spoke

Wallace Holmes wasn't exactly a man of the world. He certainly wasn't a man of many words. Some said he'd never been to Bangor, but nobody really knew that for sure. One thing everyone did know: Wallace was brilliant when it came to tinkering and fixing things. People from as far away as Prospect Harbor and even Steuben would bring their clocks, watches, lockets, and valuable trinkets all the way to West Sullivan for Wallace to fix.

Even the folks right in town claimed he was a genius.

His home and shop were on the other side of the Track Road, just across the North Sullivan Road from Duke Tracy's and sort of down behind the post office toward the river. When Wallace would go up to the store to get his mail or buy some cookies and milk or something, he'd walk with his arms straight down at his sides. They'd never move. If anyone spoke to him, he'd answer, "G'day." Period. Wallace had nothing more to say.

The only variation in these trips were the rare occasions when he'd ride his bike to the store, and that sight was worth the price of admission. The wheels on it were thin but huge. And the seat was so high he must have stood on a ladder to mount it. Yessir, that bicycle was like something out of a 1920 catalog. But Wallace had built it himself, and once he got out to the tarred road, it would really smoke.

If you had problems with your own bike—I mean major stuff, with the sprocket or something—your mother would tell you, "Go see if Wallace Holmes can fix it." Which was easy for her to say, since she'd never had to try communicating with the man.

One day, the pedals on my bike wouldn't turn, meaning that there was something wrong with a major part. So, faced with a challenge I didn't look forward to, I headed up the road—walking and pushing and dragging the bike that wouldn't run.

As I got near the post office, Bud Joy and his daughter, Beverly, were sitting out on their lawn in the shade, so I stopped for a quick rest. That girl was so pretty I'd have liked to catch her sitting beside me at the movies, even though she was five years older. But if Marjie had found out, she'd have sent me to a monastery for sure. It would have been worse than her hearing about Dora Beane!

When I told Bud where I was taking my bike to be fixed he chuckled, teasing, "You'll be lucky if you get it back by Christmas!"

Beverly waved and said, "See you, Jack."

I kept on draggin' and pushin' that bike down the

road 'til I ended up at Wallace Holmes's front door. (Or his back door, depending on where you happened to be standing.) I yelled up to him, "Hey, Mr. Holmes, can you fix my bike?" He was sitting right there by the window working at his bench, but he didn't answer. Heck, he didn't even turn my way a skrid. So I tried it again. Still no reaction.

I decided to make one more attempt before I just left the damn bike there to rot. This time, I went up the two steps and knocked on the door. Mr. Holmes didn't even move from his stool; he just reached around, opened the door, and said, "Sit. I'll be with you," motioning me to a big leather chair. He kept working on whatever was on the bench, while I tried picking the horse hairs that were pricking me from the overstuffed chair.

The room was tiny and filled with so many clocks, watches, and tools that it was hard to believe. The tick, tick, tick sound was equally incredible. A big ol' coon cat lay sleeping on the clean linoleum floor and never moved an inch. Hanging right by the workbench was a calendar with a beautiful picture of an airplane. It was four years old—not the airplane, the calendar. Suddenly, a cuckoo clock went off, and I jumped a foot. Mr. Holmes just got off his stool and went out to my bike.

Then, a really weird thing happened: He started talking a mile a minute while he removed the rear wheel. Mr. Holmes never looked at me, but he was talking—to me—so fast it was hard to understand. Before I could say word one, he had that sprocket assembly apart and spread out in a zillion pieces on his bench. I thought, "Holy shit! I'll be in college before he gets this mother back together."

A minute later, Mr. Holmes held up a part with his long fingers and demanded in a high, shrill voice, "Why would they make this like this? Why would they put this next to the bearings?" Then he polished and oiled all the parts 'til they were bright and clean, and he put them back together—his way. Even as a kid, I remember how very impressed I was with this man.

Whenever I tried to find out how much my mother owed him, Mr. Holmes would only say, "Next time. Next time. Take your bike and go ride. It'll be faster and smoother now."

And it was. Thanks to the man who hardly ever spoke.

❧ 19 ❧

A Hot Day in West Sullivan

You take a real warm day in August, with not even a slight breeze coming off the Taunton River, and I'll tell you, mister man, that was a scorcher in downtown West Sullivan, Maine. And if you saw little beads of sweat running down Marjie's face when it wasn't even eight in the morning, you just knew it was going to be a double-header of a scorcher.

On one such day, Henry Bunker was due over to mow our field. It was a pretty good deal for him because after he did the mowing, Henry got the hay for nothing, along with the privilege of storing it in our barn until he needed it. Sometimes, however, he took a little while to get the job done. This week, he was supposed to come on Tuesday but didn't make it. After Henry didn't show up on Wednesday, he got a "Marjie Havey phone call" that evening. All I can say is that if you got my mother riled, you didn't enjoy getting a "Marjie Havey phone call." She never cursed when she was teed off, but she could make her point.

On this occasion we were having folks down for the weekend from up in Bangor, and she had promised Mort that the fields would be mowed. But, of course, Henry Bunker had been a no-show. Marjie wasn't quite fit-to-be-tied, but she couldn't have been much closer to it.

Marjie had made her point with Henry and, heat or no heat, I knew he would be driving the horses and the mowing machine across the bridge any minute now. And that was going to be a big event—not just for me.

See, on summer afternoons when Mort got home from Bangor early, we'd all jump in the car and go over to Hancock and get our milk at Henry Bunker's. My little brother, Billy, loved Henry. All the way over and all the way back we'd sing, "Henry Bunker had a farm . . . eee, iii, eee, iii, o! And on that farm he had a pig . . . eee, iii, eee, iii, o!" And we'd go on through every farm animal that ever existed. Billy was four years old then, and they say it wasn't until he was just over nineteen that he discovered there was an actual song called, "Old MacDonald."

Henry Bunker thought this little, blond-headed kid was a special kind of package. He had no fear of the horses, hogs, Holsteins, or hens on the farm. He'd get comfortable atop Henry's shoulders, and the distance from the tip of Billy's head to the ground below would measure close to eight feet. They were truly a vision together.

Needless to say, when Henry turned into our driveway with his workhorses, Lottie and Gumper, leading the way, Mom, Billy, and I were right there singin', "And on that

I sat in Henry's lap too, but I actually held the reins and got to say things like, "Gee, girl! Gee, girl!" if I wanted Lottie to turn left.

farm he had a horse . . . " Suddenly, though, scooting right up the driveway behind Henry Bunker came Mr. Buker with a carload of kids, ready to pick me up for the Sunday School Field Day out at Flander's Pond.

Can you believe it? On the hottest day of the year both Ma and I had forgotten that I had a chance to go swimming. But that left me with a tough choice because here was Henry Bunker with his horses, and he always let me and Billy drive 'em around the field! Well, that's not a hundred percent true; when it was his turn, Billy just sat in Henry's lap; when it was my turn, I did too, but I actually held the reins and got to say things like, "Gee, girl! Gee, girl!" if I wanted Lottie to turn left.

"Whichever you want to do, Jackie," said Ma. Oh sure! At night, if I wanted to stay up and listen to the radio, I got no choice. I went to bed. But now, if I wanted to help drive the team, I wouldn't get to go to a nice freshwater lake with a beach, which was quite a treat if you know how cold the salt water is around West Sullivan, Maine. On the other hand, if I went on the Sunday School Field Day, I wouldn't get to drive the horses. In the end, the thrill of haying with Henry Bunker won out.

Later, I found out that my friend Gerald Estabrook didn't have all that much fun at the pond. He lay on the sandy beach for so long that his legs were sunburned something fierce, and he couldn't even walk to the movie the next night. Of course, he tried to make me think I really "missed it" by telling me how all the guys peeked through the cracks in the old ice house and watched the girls change into their swimsuits. But Buddy Jewett claimed that was a lie, because Zelda Havey (my Aunt Zelda, who was also the Sunday-school superintendent) was right there standing guard. According to Buddy, "There warn't no free peep show for no one!"

As for me and Billy, we drove the horses, mowed the fields, and shared fried-ham-and-biscuit sandwiches from Henry Bunker's lunch bucket.

It was one fine hot day down home.

❧ 20 ❧
Snails, Spooks, and Secrets

Every year, about the time the corn was ready for picking, the older kids used to have clambakes in the evening down on the shore behind Arthur Bunker's slaughterhouse. They weren't really "clambakes" because nobody had any clams, but the older boys would get a huge bonfire going, then everyone would hunt for periwinkles (snails) and steam 'em in seaweed. When the periwinkles were cooked, they'd be partway out of their shells. Then you could stick 'em with a safety pin, dunk 'em in butter, and chew 'em up. They were very tasty, along with ears of smoked, steamed corn.

But you had to be "older" to do that kind of thing after supper—or, as Marjie would say, "You can go for a while if there's going to be a grown-up there!" Sure, Ma, all the older kids bring their mothers down to watch over things. No problem.

But then Margaret became a part of our lives, and I thought there might be a ray of hope.

A very strong, straight-up-and-down Baptist, Margaret

Orr was sixteen and not too attractive by West Sullivan standards. She wore wire-frame glasses and long dresses (always with an apron), and her hair was always pulled back in a bun. Even as a teenager, she was definitely a grown-up. Still, her arrival drew a lot of attention. The day Margaret moved in with us, all the boys—including Ding Mills, Eddy Crosby, and even Guy Jewett—dropped by to sit in our kitchen and chat it up with Ma. (Yeah, right!)

Living with us was a trade-off: Margaret got free room and board—plus three dollars a week—in return for helping Ma with a few basic cleaning chores and being pretty bossy to Billy and me. Margaret had grown up in an orphanage and needed a home, while my mother, who had developed a chronic back problem at a very early age, needed a hand with the housework. So, even though the whole thing was Mort's idea, it seemed to have merit.

I just needed to teach Margaret a few things—like how to make my breakfast on those mornings when Mom would drive up to Bangor with my father and spend the day with Aunt Louise. The kitchen arrangement was simple. I would come downstairs and sit in the rocking chair by the woodstove with my Superman comic book and a big, cold glass of milk. While I was starting to wake up, Margaret would go ahead and make my toast, in accordance with my recipe:

> ⌘ Put two pieces of bread on woodstove.
> ⌘ Turn over before they start to smoke.

⚹ Apply lots of butter to toasted side.
⚹ Cover buttered side with cinnamon and sugar.
⚹ Serve.
⚹ Repeat three times.

It was the "repeat three times" that gave the girl a conniption fit. Ma never had a problem with it, but Margaret was bent on setting a new standard for my morning routine. As in, "Two slices of cinnamon toast is enough for anyone!" On other mornings, she'd just glare at me while she sat at the kitchen table eating her Rice Krispies and Ma allowed me to gorge on eight or even ten pieces of cinnamon toast. Didn't I love to make Margaret glare!

But, if she was an old biddy in some ways, she was awfully good to all of us during her four years as part of our family. She would do things like help me get furnace wood into the cellar after Monty Williams had cut it up with his bucksaw. She'd pitch right in and load up the wheelbarrow with the biggest chunks; haul the stuff through the shed and into the barn; then unload the wood and carry it piece by piece through the kitchen, through the dining room, and down the cellar stairs.

And what stairs they were! They led into a dark dungeon where one dim light hung from the ceiling and big black spiders crawled all over the place. As if that wasn't bad enough—this is no lie—the place was filled with real spooks. If you want proof, just listen to this: My great-grandfather, Moore, who was bedridden for two years with a broken hip, died in the upstairs room that was directly over the cellar woodpile. While he was alive, he kept a cane with an orange glass handle in the small closet right next to his bed.

One rainy summer afternoon, years after he died, me and Buddy Jewett borrowed that cane to use as a sword, and somehow it got lost out in the haymow. A few months later, on a winter night when I had to go down into the cellar and bank the fire before bed, I heard a woman in the woodpile laughing her crazy head off. Then, there was Gramp Moore, right in the darkest end of the cellar, limping around on the dirt floor with no cane! I couldn't speak . . . I couldn't say word one. The old man shook his fist at me while I just stood there and peed my pants. How much more proof of real spooks do you need than that?

So, when ol' Margaret said she'd help me lug in the wood and stack it in the cellar, I figured that since she was a girl, she'd get scared as hell if I told her what was really going on down there. Then, I'd be on my own with the job. For once, I kept my mouth shut.

In my mother's eyes, Margaret was about as pure grown-up as grown-up could be. So, whether there was an all-day outing at the beach or an evening clambake down on the riverbank, I could go as long as Margaret was going. Believe me, the resulting negotiations had a very real impact on the development of my approach to people and events during the years to come. For example, I'd say, "Hey Margaret! Boy, do you look nice today. Going up to

Margaret was awfully good to all of us during her four years as part of our family.

the clambake tonight? I hear they're gonna have a great cookout and free Kool-Aid. Mom says I can go as long as you're gonna be there, too."

The Response: "Don't keep pestering me, Jack. Right now I have a splitting headache, and just the thought of all that walking after supper makes me feel even worse."

The Truth: Margaret can hardly wait to go the clambake, but she's gonna keep me dangling about it all day.

The Lesson: Don't get Margaret riled-up for no reason at all. It'll come back to haunt you.

The Bottom Line: Settle for two pieces of cinnamon toast in the morning, even when Marjie is getting breakfast. It'll show character.

❧ 21 ❧

Firecrackers and Teddy Bears

Our dog, Satan, always had one unadulterated bad time on the Fourth of July. He hated the sound of guns. So, naturally, he hated the sound of fireworks. If just one tiny ladyfinger went off, Sate was outta there! He'd hightail it into the barn or shed where no one would see him 'til the celebration was over. Uncle Dwight always claimed it was because Sate's straight-up ears were so sensitive.

But for the rest of us—including other dogs, cats, and people—the Fourth was second only to Christmas in terms of major fun. And this year the celebration was going to be doubly major.

Things started happening about a week before Flag Day, when Dwight showed up from work with two long pieces of iron pipe in the trunk of the car. Me and Keith dragged 'em out, and laid 'em down on the path between the barn and the woodpile—the one that led directly out to the family's hog pen. Then it started getting dark.

No matter. Uncle Dwight was taking two vacation

days from his job at the Green Front, and construction of the new horseshoe court would start right there between the barn and the woodpile the next morning—rain or shine.

There were quite a few places around West Sullivan where you could pitch horseshoes. One was even as close by as the area behind Bobby Black's garage. Then there was that court up by Duke's house, but the apple tree branches had started to grow around it at one end, and nobody used it anymore. Besides, this new one that we were about to construct was going to be "official," meaning the court had to be ten feet wide by fifty feet long with a six-foot-square pitcher's box at each end and an iron stake, stuck into clay, in the center of each pit. The distance from stake to stake? Exactly forty feet.

For most people in town, a game of horseshoes was just that: a game. And that's the way it had always been for my Uncle Dwight. The only difference was that almost nobody ever beat him at it. Until last summer. Dwight entered the Maine State Championship matches and went all the way to the semifinals held at Toddy's Pond. There he took a lickin' from Maynard Barnes, a trucker from Orland and the man who went on to win the championship and the trophy.

Some say that from that day on, when Dwight wasn't hunting or fishing, he spent every waking minute thinking about making his comeback.

That year, the Fourth of July was on a Saturday. On

Once he got his horseshoe court built to perfection, it was practice, practice, and more practice for Uncle Dwight.

the very next day, the Maine State Horseshoe Championship finals would be held up in Brewer. You want double fun during just one weekend, mister man? You got it! In the meantime, once he got his horseshoe court built to perfection, it was practice, practice, and more practice for Uncle Dwight.

He pitched a turn-and-a-quarter shoe that was a thing of beauty to watch. He'd float ringer on top of ringer on top of ringer. The shoe would sail through the air just like it had eyes—straight, soft, and turning smoothly. Then there'd be a clang! and, seconds later, another clang! Just like clockwork. All the boys in town would show up to give Dwight a game. The results: 21–zip, 21–zip, 21–zip.

The only thing was, Maynard Barnes had equal skills, and he was the man to beat if Dwight was to put that trophy on his mantle. And did he ever want it!

Some say if it hadn't been for Phil and Dave Havey, he would have practiced right through the Fourth. But, like Mort and Dwight himself, these were sons of the Brothers Five and, therefore, special. Phil and Dave had both grown up in the third Havey house, the one next door to Peter and Mrs. Mills and the one that was now totally run down, with all its windows broken and the like. At an age, they had both moved away and settled in Connecticut, where Phil became an engineer and Dave went to work as a state cop.

These two always came back home for the Fourth . . . and they always came loaded with "The Fireworks." Now,

I'm not talkin' about the little stuff that was sold in Ellsworth and Bangor. I'm talkin' major skyrockets, huge roman candles, and cherry bombs that would blow the roof off a chicken coop. On the Friday before the Fourth, old friends from all over would gather in our kitchen to drink beer, tell the wildest stories you ever heard, and sing songs into the middle of the night.

The next morning, whoever sobered-up first would go out in the driveway, light a cherry bomb under a tin can, and blow the hell out of it. That meant, as the saying goes, "Let the games begin!" This year was no exception, and we all had more fun than you can shake a stick at.

The day after the Fourth, Keith, Jody, and me got Dwight to promise that "win, lose, or draw" at the tournament, we would stop at Grant's Drug Store in Hancock on the way home for an ice-cream soda. Then we piled into the Chevy with Uncle Dwight and headed for Brewer Flats and the Maine State Horseshoe Championship. We were a pretty excited bunch.

But that didn't last long.

Lemme tell you, this event was like watching grass grow. Worse, they had three horseshoe courts out in the middle of a field with no shade around anywhere, and it was hotter than a skunk. The closest thing to a refreshment stand was a cold-water hose hooked up to a barn down the road a ways.

About fifty players, including Uncle Dwight and Maynard Barnes, had entered the "play-'til-you-lose" tournament. Plus there must have been another hundred people just milling around in the dusty field waiting for the next match. Jody's ongoing question to nobody in particular was, "When will it be over?" Keith stayed with it, but after six hours me and Jody got in the back seat of the car and fell asleep. On the way home, she woke up for a minute to ask who won, to which Keith replied, "In case anyone is interested, your father is now the new State of Maine Horseshoe Pitching Champion." I thought I heard Jody say, "Oh."

Later, I opened an eye briefly as we went by Grant's Drug Store in Hancock. It was closed up tighter 'n a teddy bear.

❦ 22 ❦

Bangor and Bullies

Uncle Dwight's victory over Maynard Barnes wasn't the only big event of that summer.

The storm windows on our West Sullivan house had seen their last winter. One more turn of one more screw was going to find nothing but wood rot. And the uninsulated furnace provided more heat for the spooks in the cellar than for the people upstairs. Our house was a great family home in the summer, but living there year round was starting to be all too costly on my father's annual income of less than $1,500. I began to hear Marjie and Mort whispering about renting a place in Bangor during the winter.

Moving didn't strike me as being the end of the world. The previous winter, during Christmas vacation, Mom, Billy, and me had spent a week in Bangor with Aunt Louise, Uncle Wally, and Cousin Bob. We had lost our heat in West Sullivan, and Billy about froze his nose off. In truth, according to Doc Black, Billy did freeze his nose, but Marjie said I shouldn't go around braggin' about it.

I didn't hate Bangor at all. Bob and me had great fun
there. For instance on snowy nights, just before supper,
we'd hang on the back of trolley cars and see how far we
could go for free. A ride from Palm Street all the way out
to the Garland Street turn was our best for the week. That
evening when we got back to Aunt Louise's all covered
with snow, I thought Marjie was gonna have a bird. She
wasn't much into city stuff, but there was lots to do.

In West Sullivan, even the Alhambra closed during
the winter months, while in Bangor there were three
different movie houses going straight out, including the
Park Theater, which had a double feature on Saturday
afternoons—two full-length movies plus a cartoon! So, if
Mort and Marjie wanted to whisper about going to the
city, that was fine with me. Besides it was just talk, right?

Wrong. That year, Labor Day wasn't the only thing to
come and go. We went, too, from West Sullivan to a rental
house on outer Palm Street in Bangor. Come May, we'd be
heading back home, and for the time being this place
didn't look all that bad. There were no spooks in the
cellar—just a coal bin, and that was gonna be Mort's baby.
(Later, I did enjoy sitting on the cellar stairs, watching the
deliverymen fill the bin by shoveling the stuff through a
window and sliding it down a long metal chute. That was
a new treat for me.)

The Jones family lived directly across the street, and
there were two brothers about a year apart. The Joneses
were Chinese, which was also a treat for me since there

weren't any Chinese families in West Sullivan. The youngest boy, Donald, was my age and he was a very special artist for a kid of eight years old. Donald could draw anything, and the teacher always held up his work in class.

Which reminds me of my first day at the Mary S. Snow School in Bangor. It was horrible—my mother insisted on taking me! Sure, she had to sign me up, but can you imagine what it's like when your own mother walks you into a new school and all the kids are staring at you like you were a little baby or something? I instantly got homesick for West Sullivan, where everybody knew everybody and going to school on the bus was like being with good friends every morning.

The Wallaces (Aunt Louise, Uncle Wally, and Cousin Bob) lived close by on Elm Street, and during the school lunch hour I'd go over to play tag football in the street with Herby Follett and Eddy Shapleigh. Bob was a grade up from me, but he went to Mary Snow, too, so we always walked to school together. Normally we took the shortcut through the city dump.

There was always something burning and smoking in there—like old tires, rags, or cardboard boxes—and if the wind was coming the wrong way, your eyes might burn and water up. The rats that were running around never scared us. When we had time before the next-to-last bell at school, we'd stop and throw old cans and things at 'em.

Bruce Trenholm. He was what scared us!

I used to lie awake at night thinking about him beating us up on the way home from school. Bruce was in my class, but he'd stayed back a year and was a lot bigger than Bobby or me. My mother probably thought of him as "a nice young boy" because he was always so bright and shiny clean that he looked like he had been scrubbed down with a wire brush. But he was a mean, mean kid.

He loved to get way ahead of us along the dump path then jump out from behind an old box or mattress or something, swearing and yelling and punching us on the back and shoulders. He'd run after us laughing and screaming until he had to turn off and go in another direction. Too bad for us that our friend Herby Follett went to parochial school. He was small but tougher 'n nails, and he could have whipped Bruce Trenholm in an eye-blink.

It was just me and Bobby against the world, and obviously we needed a plan of attack. What we came up with was pretty simple: The next time we saw Bruce at the dump, I'd jump on him and hold his arms and Bob would hit him and hit him and hit him until he bled and yelled "uncle."

That Friday, Bob and me were about halfway through the dump on the way home from school when Bruce ambushed us. And true to our plan, I jumped him, hopping right on his back and pinning his arms to his sides. Then, untrue to our plan, Bobby put his head down and ran like a sonuvabitch for home.

Someone, somewhere, sometime must have written something that describes my exact feelings at being alone, hanging onto the back of the school bully, in the middle of the city dump on that particular afternoon. But I've never read it.

It took ol' Bruce about half a second to fling me to the ground and announce that if I got up before the rats ate me, he'd come back and kill me straight-out dead. By the time I dared to head home, the street lights were on and I sure wasn't looking forward to going back to school when Monday rolled around. But I did. And a strange thing happened during "basement break." I was standing in line at the water fountain when I felt a soft slap on the back of my head. When I turned around I was looking directly into ol' Bruce's chuckling face.

"Gonna beat up on me again today, Jack?" he asked with a laugh.

I answered, "No Bruce."

And you know something? He and I became very, very good friends after that.

❧ 23 ☙

Crime in
the Streets

On Columbus Day, October 12, 1937, me and Satan had decided to hike downtown and pay a visit to Aunt Dora at The Women's Hat Shop on Central Street. It was still early in the morning when we got there, and the long, green shade on her front door was pulled all the way down. I figured she was out back working, so we stood there while I knocked and knocked but got no answer.

The walk up to the *Bangor Commercial* was only another five minutes, so we headed across the Kenduskeag Mall Bridge just in time to hear the workers' jackhammers and drills start up around the slight bend in Central Street. The noise was so loud it hurt my ears and true to form, it sent Sate shooting like hell up Park Street, headed for home. I yelled for him to come back but never had a chance.

So I went on alone, and once I rounded the bend I couldn't believe the awful scene in front of Dakin's Sporting Goods store. Two guys were lying on the trolley-car tracks like they had been hit by a truck. Even worse for me was seeing firemen with hoses, washing blood down the gutters of Central Street. The "jackhammering" I had heard was FBI agents firing their machine guns at a bunch of bandits. Now that the noise had stopped, people were running around like crazy. I grabbed a man by the arm, and he told me that the G-men had just killed a bandit called Al Brady, plus his sidekick. Right there in front of Dakin's.

Did I ever hightail it for the *Commercial* newsroom. I mean this was big-time Chicago stuff, not what usually happened in downtown Bangor, Maine, on Columbus Day. After I told the editor, a.k.a. Mort Havey, what had happened, the *Commercial* beat the *News* to a first edition with this once-in-a-lifetime story by about five minutes.

Luckily, my own brush with crime never made the front page of either newspaper.

I used to go into the J. J. Newberry five-and-dime in Bangor, pick up a few things that cost less than a quarter, and just walk out the door with the stuff in my pocket. It was a kind of game me and my friend Paul Aloes used to play on Saturday mornings. Paul had just moved to Bangor from Lawrence, Massachusetts, and we were in the same third-grade room at Mary Snow. Partly because both of us were "from away," we became real good buddies, and we both enjoyed stealing. Small stuff, that is.

Except for the one evening when we got The Big Idea.

It all started when we were standing outside the open windows of the Nissen Bakery down on Central Street, watching the big round balls of raw dough going up the conveyor belt. We went there a lot, and the workers, who enjoyed kidding us, would toss us little scraps of the dough through the open windows. It was tasty eating, but on this particular night we were both starved, and the smell of that baking bread had us begging the workers for a whole loaf of the real stuff.

One of 'em came over to the window ledge to light up a smoke, and he whispered, "Just slip into the garage." It was connected to the bakery, and we just pushed open the sliding door about a foot, revealing—are you ready for this?—racks of unsliced loaves just sitting there cooling. In a flash, there were two fewer, and me and Paul were out of the garage and across the street onto someone's lawn, where we sat down and broke into the warm, uncut crusts of our mouth-watering booty. Gawd, was it ever good.

But as we sat there jawing and tearing big hunks of soft, freshly baked bread out of the middle of the warm crusts, I told Paul that inside my loaf there was a huge chunk of butter and that it was melting all over the bread. I was just joking, but in seconds we both came up with an idea. And this was The Big Idea.

We knew that a new supermarket had just opened down on Harlow Street, which was right over the hill if we took a shortcut. And did they have butter there? You bet.

The store's Grand Opening was still going on, so the place was pretty crowded. Paul was wearing a tight, zippered windbreaker, and I had my big winter mackinaw on. We figured that I could keep watch while he stuffed the butter under my coat, allowing me to hold it with my hands pushed down into my pockets. It was a done deal.

Almost.

Store Manager (looking straight at the front of my coat): "Hi fellas, can I help you with something?"

Me: "Nope. Just leaving."

Store Manager (still looking straight at the front of my coat): "Well, I guess you found what you wanted."

Paul: "No, we were just looking around the new store, sir."

Store Manager: "Really? You boys live around here? (Now my heart is beating like a two-dollar drum, and I know he hears it!)

Me: "Yessa, right here in Bangor."

Store Manager (looking even more intently at the front of my coat): "Fine. But I don't ever want to see either one of you back in my store again. Is that clear? Never! Not today! Not tomorrow. Not before the end of the world. Are you hearing me?"

Me and Paul: "Yes sir. Thank you, sir. G'night, sir."

Heading for home, we both seemed to have lost our appetites, so we agreed to hide the butter in some bushes behind Bangor High School and go back for it the next day. But we never did. Neither of us ever wanted to be reminded again of The Big Idea.

Paul, however, did contend that making us promise to stay out of the store until the "end of the world" was a pretty grumpy reaction to a pretty minor crime.

⤙ 24 ⤚
Loved Ones

You're not going to believe what I'm about to tell you. In fact, you'll probably just turn away and say, "This could have never happened to an eight-year-old kid." But it did.

I fell in love

So help me God, I fell in love with a girl who was right in my very own classroom. She had long brown hair and beautiful eyes, and she was only three or four inches taller than me. We really didn't meet or talk 'til the afternoon when I saw her at the skating pond over in Broadway Park. I had racing skates—the ones with the long blades. So I could go a lot faster than most kids and throw a pretty good spray of ice and snow when I put on the brakes.

When I skated by her and a group of her girlfriends, she said, "Oh, Jack, I love your skates," I stopped and almost melted a hole in the ice. In search of words, I blabbered something about being able to beat almost anyone around in a race to the other end of the pond. She answered simply, "Let's go!"

Okay, so she beat me by ten feet or so. Who cares? I now had a talking thing going with the girl I was going to marry: Kaye Trenholm, my first real love. No, she wasn't Bruce Trenholm's sister; she was his cousin.

Right under the evil eye of our teacher, Miss Hinckley, we started passing notes back and forth in school. Kaye sat in the row of desks next to the windows while I sat way over on the other side of the classroom, almost up against the blackboards. Smirky little Miss Goodie Two-Shoes, a.k.a. Myra McCann, was squarely between us, in the middle row. Knowing that "She Who Never Did Anything Wrong" would not hand my notes along to Kaye, I passed them over to Eugene Gonyar, who sat behind Myra. Gene would palm the note and go to the front of the room to sharpen his pencil, then make the drop to Kaye on his way back. Most often I got Kaye's loving response in a handoff at the drinking fountain during the basement break. Our romantic exchanges would go something like this:

Me to Kaye: "Going skating after school?"

Kaye to me: "Have to go to dentist."

But I always saved all her notes and tucked 'em under my mattress at the rented house on Palm Street. She just lived over on Essex Street, which wasn't far, so I started walking to school that way. Sometimes we'd meet up and sort of walk along together—as in, I'd walk way ahead, then she'd run up from behind and push me into a snowbank. I'd get up and chase her the rest of the way to the iron railing that surrounded the Mary Snow school-yard.

But Kaye Trenholm wasn't the only woman in my life that winter. It was getting close to one of my very favorite times of year—when my Grandmother Havey would come visit us for two weeks.

Gram Havey was a pistol. She was the widow of Harvard Hannah Havey, one of the famed "Brothers Five." Gram had left Maine shortly after my grandfather died. During their years together, she had a great reputation for being a big spender. They say that if Harvard gave her $100 for a shopping trip in Ellsworth, she'd spend it all at the five-and-dime, not buying a thing that cost more than a quarter.

Though he was an early-on king of the granite business, Gramp Havey saw his North Sullivan company, Crabtree & Havey, fall into bankruptcy in 1933. So when he died, Gram didn't have two nickels to rub together. But that part of it all never bothered her. Rich or poor, she loved life and had the laugh and good nature to prove it. Shortly after Harvard "went south," so did Gram—to North Attleboro, Massachusetts. There she had somehow gotten hooked up with a Miss Abendroth, a wealthy spinster who needed a live-in cook.

Miss A., a funny little lady with an English accent, not only got herself the best live-in cook east of the Rockies, she gained a loving companion for life. Those two were absolute soul buddies. And they were truly a sight to see as they drove around Attleboro together in what Miss Abendroth called her "flivvie." Miss A. would be behind the wheel, slightly bent and weighing in at about eighty-five pounds with her winter boots and coat on. Next to her in the front seat would be Gram Havey, just under six feet tall and straight as a ramrod. The two of 'em would be laughing up a storm. They always were.

They would part only for four weeks a year, during February, when Miss A. would take the train to her winter home in Palm Beach, Florida, and Gram would opt to return home to Maine for the month. She'd spend two weeks with Dwight and his family, and two weeks with us. This winter, of course, we had closed up our West Sullivan house, the place where she had lived her entire married life, the home where she had raised both Mort and Dwight. But she never moaned or bitched a peep about it, because Martha Havey was one special lady.

And now we had her with us, right here in Bangor, for two whole weeks!

Early in the morning, I'd wake up and see the light shining under her door. I couldn't get going fast enough. She'd be reading in bed and would tell me, "It's only four o'clock, so snuggle in here with Gram and get yourself a few more winks." (My grandmother would regularly play cards—bridge, canasta, solitaire, you name it— 'til eleven at night, but she'd still never sleep past four in the morning.)

By five, I'd reawaken, and she'd tell me stories about when she was a little girl—then Martha Moore—growing up down in Steuben. This year, I told her that someday I'd be marrying Kaye Trenholm. She thought that was nice as long as I didn't rush into it. (If I had shared the news with my own mother, she'd have broken out in a henhouse rash.)

Come five-thirty, me and Gram would go downstairs, have breakfast, then head into the dining room for the first card game of the day. For some reason, when my mother got up and came downstairs, it frosted her that at only seven o'clock we'd been playing canasta for more than an hour.

Ma loved Gram Havey, but I always sensed that there might have been a little jealousy in the kitchen. See, when it came to cooking, Marjie couldn't fry a fruit fly, while Gram could whip up the best stuff you ever tasted without measuring a thing. You wanted truffles? You got truffles. You wanted croissants? You got croissants. You wanted buttermilk doughnuts? You got buttermilk doughnuts.

Most important, when Gram finished cooking, she'd leave all the dirty dishes in the sink, relax, and have a good game of cards. Marjie, of course, couldn't stand one dirty dish in the sink for one minute. So you might say this was "the straw that broke the camel's back," so to speak. (I sure as hell wouldn't say it, but you might.)

Come the end of February, Gram left on schedule to go back to North Attleboro. Not long after that, Sate died. So, I had to say good-bye not only to my grandmother but to my first, my closest, and my most ever-loving buddy who always slept by my bed.

For a lotta, lotta nights I just cried myself to sleep.

25

Going Home

Our long-awaited move back to West Sullivan happened on the first Saturday in June. Miss Hinckley, my teacher at the Mary Snow School, had allowed that my marks were good enough that she could pass me along to the next grade two weeks early. So, after making the trip in Mort's Ford coupe, I was back home and free as a bird.

The moving van arrived in West Sullivan two hours late, the crew telling how they had broken down twice after leaving Bangor. By the looks of their truck, you could believe it.

Right after they pulled in, Gerald Estabrook came up the gravel driveway like a rocket on his Iver Johnson bike with the headlight that never worked. It was good to see him. Jody had come running across the field earlier to give me a big motherly hug and kiss. Only a year older than me, she still had that way about her. Everyone was saddened about Sate, and wouldn't you know, I up and started cryin' again. But then they pulled my ol' Olympia bike out of the van, and me and Gerald shot off, racing up the North Sullivan Road, almost like nothing had changed.

Our destination was the top of the hill and Willie Havey's store, where we both got ourselves a big, cold bottle of Sun Spot orange soda, which we took out on the shaded front steps to drink. Sun Spot was the biggest soda you could buy for a nickel, and the trick was to see who could belch the first and the loudest. It was really no contest, since I had perfected the Wayne "Ding" Mills method of just pouring a bottled drink down my throat, without swallowing, 'til I burped. Gerald had a lot to learn.

We sat and chatted, but my stories about Bangor didn't interest him much. Then I told him I had learned how to deal cards off the bottom of the deck. Gerald said that was nothing, that he knew a card trick only Houdini himself could figure out. Plus, back in November, his father had bought him a single-shot .22 bolt-action Marlin rifle for his very own. He said, "Top that!" and I couldn't.

Which was about the time two North Sullivan boys we both knew pulled up on their bikes. They were on the way into the store. They said hi to Gerald and hi to me, but they didn't use my name. Gerald yelled out that the last Superman comic book had been bought, and when they came back out, the three of 'em gabbed it up for awhile. It was like I wasn't even there, and a very weird feeling crept up my back.

Was I a freakin' Summer Person or something? Was I now a kid who lived in Bangor and only came down for the summer? That's not the way I saw it. I was a West

Sullivan native who, for family-money reasons, had to knock around Bangor for a few months during the winter 'til we could all come back home knowing the house would stay pretty warm without the furnace.

That night, when I slid into my own bed for the first time in months, nobody had to tell me where home was. I knew that in the morning, I'd lean up on my elbow and look out the window—across the highway, across the ballfield—at that beautiful river, and the world would be just fine. The only thing missing would be Sate lying there with me.

And that was always gonna be a big miss.

J.